Spirit Fed Entrepreneur:
Grow Your Business with a Fearless Mindset

Compiled by Jayne Rios

Featured Author: Sandi Mitchell

DEDICATION

This book is dedicated to God and Christian Entrepreneurs throughout the world. For those with ears let them hear, for those with eyes let them see. God is leading His people from fear-based living into a better way of life. He needs workers because the harvest is many. This book is dedicated to Spirit Fed Entrepreneurs who listen, act and move...changing the world for the better!

CONTENT

ACKNOWLEDGMENTS

Thank you Spirit Fed Entrepreneur Authors for sharing your life and business stories in the hope of encouraging others to live out their passion. Thank each of you for your service to others.

To Bill and Jill Mitchell: Thank you, Dad, for teaching me about the entrepreneurial spirit. And thank you, Mom, for teaching me about a joy-filled life. I love you both very much!

1. INTRODUCTION

Entrepreneurs have a multitude of choices and decisions to make every day. Whether these decisions we make are conscious or unconscious, they affect the outcome of tomorrow and many days after that. Being indecisive is as much of a choice as a well-thought out decision, and sometimes that indecision has more of an impact on business than a conscious choice.

We can choose to continue what we are doing and receive the same results. We can choose defeat, or we can choose victory. We can choose to be grateful, or we can choose to complain. We can choose to procrastinate, making two tasks last all day, or we can choose to meet our tasks head on. It's the everyday choices we make in life that determine our next steps.

What hinders our choice for success?

One of the major stumbling blocks to becoming a confident entrepreneur is fear. One of my mentors said: "What you think is what you are." Henry Ford said, "Whether you think you can or think you can't, you are right!" In other words, your thoughts have power, and if you think positive thoughts, positive results will follow. If you think fearful thoughts, your fears will become your reality.

Most of our fears are imagined fears; they are not dangerous or painful. Even so, they are a perceived threat, such as a threat to finances, ego, family, business or a relationship. It's real to us because it's a "what if" scenario. For the most part, those "what if" moments never come, but we waste tons of energy on the threat. The goal is to eliminate those "what if" fears and move forward toward confidence.

Here's a quick exercise for you if fear is one of your confidence-robbers:

Divide a piece of paper into four columns. In the first column list everything you fear at this very moment. In the second column write down the worst thing that could happen if that fear came to pass. In the third column note the best that could happen. In the final column indicate if the fear is real or imagined.

Definition of Fear: An unpleasant emotion caused by the belief that someone or something is dangerous, likely to cause pain or a threat.

Definition of Confident: A pleasant emotion caused by the belief that we are protected, safe, loved and most of all grateful for where we are, who we are and what's to come.

Moving Forward

In today's society I hear so many people asking the 'universe' to provide, maybe this is because of books like The Secret or The Power of Now. These are great books, but as a Christian, I have a hard time talking to the universe when I know God created the universe. I also know that God alone provides, according to His Will.

All of the authors in this book have relied on the one true Power in the universe to succeed in business. We have listened to the Spirit, we have acted on Faith and we have Moved according to our belief. Our belief is that we are Children of God and if He is for us who could ever come against us! We have learned to overcome the unhealthy fear that so many Entrepreneurs fall prey to and now we are sharing our stories with you. Our mission is to raise up Christian Entrepreneurs to their Highest Potential!

Enjoy these true stories!

2. MAKE A CHOICE FOR SPIRIT FED LIVING
BY JAYNE RIOS

Every choice we make affects the outcome of tomorrow. Every move we make is a result of a choice we make. Choices and outcomes are the result of what we are thinking. What we think is a choice we make. The choices you make today will affect your outcome for tomorrow, good or bad.

Wow, I wish I would have known that 20 years ago. It's taken a long time to learn those lessons. But I have learned them. And as my Grandmother would say, "You've come a long way baby!". I could go into detail about my life story and the many sorrows and challenges I had to face as a child, teenager and young adult; suffice it to say it wasn't the best. What hurt *me* most looking back, was me, my attitude about what was going around me and ultimately the horrible choices I made. My excuse was to escape my issues instead of reaching out and learning from others and being more open minded to change.

Rosebud

My nickname was Rosebud growing up. My mom called me that almost every day. I use to love it until I was 35 and realized I was just now becoming a blooming rose. Honestly, I really should have been a blooming rose in my 20's. But here I am in my mid 30's and just realizing my full potential and what I was intended to be; a loving, caring, thoughtful person with strength, dignity and a bright future in front of me. How the choices I made in life would have been so much better if I had only known this before.

You see a Rosebud is beautiful, but it's closed. It hides inside itself for protection and shelter, it's comfortable in there. Its petals are not exposed, so not to get withered by the storm. It doesn't and can't reach out to anyone for help because it doesn't know how to open and be exposed. Trust is a very difficult thing to do for the Rosebud. If it doesn't open, it thinks it is safe.

The truth is the Rosebud wants to open because that is what it was made to do, but it doesn't know which petal to open first. If it exposes one petal will it need to expose them all? Will there be other roses out there like it? Can it protect itself from the storm if exposed?

These are a lot of issues I related to as the Rosebud. My head told me that no one was going through or went through what I did. I saw one crowd and thought, "I am not as good as they are, they won't understand me". I saw my girlfriends had really great family lives and I could see the difference and always compared my life to theirs. Of course they loved me for me, but not until I was a Blooming Rose did I realize that. I felt less than other people, it was a bad feeling. And of course my head played along, I would stop myself before I started, I would second guess myself in everything I did, I let others' opinions sway me left then right, I was a people pleaser always looking out for the other person but neglecting myself. This went on for over 20 years. Needless to say the choices I was making were not of sound mind.

The other day a friend and I were talking about a situation I was in resulting from a choice I made 17 years ago and she said, "Well it's the choice you made." I told her, "Yes, but that choice was a result of my environment, not being of sound mind, and not being capable of making 'good, positive' choices for myself." So now I had the choice, to end it or make the best of it. I was choosing to turn it around and make the best of it...but I still have a choice. No matter what age, you have a choice.

The Rosebud must take it day by day, moment by moment. Each petal must open and begin feeling its worth. Day by day it makes the choice to get up, move and open itself to the elements of this world. Each day it gets more strength to open more petals and trust more. Every new element is a precious gift and a valuable lesson. Raindrops become its best friend...in those storms it learns its greatest lessons and receives more strength. In the sunshine it learns to feel joy, love, peace and hope. It strives each day to become a fully developed Blooming Rose.

Blooming Rose

A Blooming Rose, which I proudly call myself today, is open and free, feels beautiful on the inside and is not afraid to show it off. It's open to the outside air, sunshine and all of the weather elements. It's learned that nobody's life is perfect and it's okay to make mistakes. It's open and honest about its life and every petal is a precious trophy. Every petal is unique and with every rain drop is a valuable lesson. The Blooming Rose knows its value and realizes every day is a precious moment, so it enjoys itself; dancing in the wind and sending out sweet fragrance for all who come near.

What I have learned working with my clients is that no matter your age, you can become a Blooming Rose. It starts with believing in yourself, connecting with the right people, and learning the secret to turning off negativity in your head by switching it with positive thoughts. A Blooming Rose knows the power within itself and it isn't afraid to show it and share it.

Skip Ahead, I am 47 a Full Blown Rose

The past 10 years living as a full blown rose have been incredible! I have many friends, I have built 3 companies, I have 2 great kids I get to spend every day with, a fabulous husband and I could go on (but for time sake I will stop:-). I have allowed myself to be free and to love and to let people in. So many new opportunities have opened up for me and it continues to this day. The choices I make daily are in sound mind and I allow myself to say no and feel fine about it (that's a great feeling in itself, try it). I choose to wake up thankful. I choose to go to bed thankful. Being grateful for what I have has been a huge step in helping me feel really good about my life. When I was in Africa videotaping an eLearning course I realized VERY quickly how lucky and blessed we are to live in the United States. When kids are walking down the street with no shoes on their feet and mom's crying because their babies are dying from malaria and no one can do anything...it's time to look in the mirror and make a choice. Complain or be Grateful. Make a good choice each day, choose to be positive and watch the difference it will make in your life.

Try these steps, this was my path:

Read. Learn from others, you are not alone. We have many resources to assist us with resolving our past and why we act like we do. My number one choice: The Bible. It has many verses to help with low self-esteem, abuse, unforgiveness, anger, bitterness, fear.

Open yourself to new opportunities. Write down your goals and visualize it, feel it and live a life moving toward your goals every day.   When you open yourself emotionally people feel they can connect with you.

Stop thinking negative thoughts. Write down a few things/people/places and Scripture that make you happy and make you feel good about yourself. When you start to feel or think negative thoughts, remember your list, pick one, memorize a Verse and focus on that until you feel better. Replace negative with positive.

Elevate your thinking. Always remember the long-term goal.

Write goals, open up for new opportunities, start thinking positive thoughts and keep your eye on the prize. Everything else is short-term. Stay positive.

Practice, Practice, Practice! Make a choice for positive Spirit Fed change today and change your world the better!

> **"Peace I leave with you; My peace I give to you; not as the world gives but as I give to you. Do not let your heart be troubled, nor let it be fearful." --Jesus**

ABOUT JAYNE RIOS

Jayne Rios has 25 years' experience in TV and marketing. She is the CEO & co-Founder of WGLA: Women's Global Leadership Alliance, President and Founder of WBTVN Women's Broadcast Television Network and CEO and Founder of Spirit Fed Institute. She is passionate about helping others achieve the success she has earned.

Jayne is author of The Interactive Author: Monetize Your Message, compiler and author of Spirit Fed Entrepreneur and co-author of Pure Wealth, Networking to Increase Your Net Worth, The Unsinkabable Soul and Change Your World.

For anyone ready to incorporate God into their business or those who are ready to eliminate unhealthy fear and move forward visit http://www.spiritfedlife.com.

CONTACT JAYNE RIOS

Begin living the life you want. Visit our website for a free offer: http://www.spiritfedbook.com or to host your own television show within our Spirit Fed Network visit http://www.womensbroadcasttv.com.

Contact Links:

Email: jayne@godfident.com

Phone: 817-480-3485

Websites: http://www.spiritfedlife.com and http://www.womensgla.com and http://www.womensbroadcasttv.com

Facebook:

Like our Page at: https://www.facebook.com/spiritfedmindset

Visit Jayne's personal page and connect at: https://www.facebook.com/acts2technology and join our Global Network at: https://www.facebook.com/groups/womensgloballeadershipallianc e/
Twitter: http://www.twitter.com/SpiritFedLife

LinkedIn: http://www.linkedin.com/in/jaynerios

3. FEARLESSNESS
BY SANDI MITCHELL

I was shocked to hear those words said to me that I, as a leader, had been scripted to say a few times before, "Sandi, we are eliminating your position. You have three weeks to find other employment within the company if you so choose."

My first thought was, "Wait. What? Me?" I was turning 50 that year. I'd been with the company 17 years. I was leading a global training group. They were just kidding, right?

Then, my second thought was, "Woo hoo!" I'd been with the company 17 years – which means a great severance and bonus. They paid for my MBA and my Executive Coaching certification. They trained me to be Chief of Staff in Legal and HR, and they gave me the opportunity to create a corporate university responsible for 4200 people in 46 countries! I was ready to spread my wings and fly!

For the next three weeks, I bounced back and forth between fear and excitement. And then, I was on my own. I chose my company name. I created an office in the back bedroom. I hung out my shingle for executive coaching. And I waited.

And waited.   ...   And waited!

Then, I realized, it would probably be easier to get clients if I went outside of my great little home office and met people. So, I did. I went to every networking event, listened to every webinar, and joined every group I could find. Only to realize there is so much noise out there and until I knew who I could help the most, I couldn't find them, and they couldn't find me. So, I stopped.

And prayed.

And found the one voice that mattered. I decided God is the CEO of my company. I'm the President. And together, we make this business exactly what it is meant to be. I find that when I have consistent board meetings every morning (prayer time!) and listen, not just ask for what I want, then the business is very solid. And when I tend to wander off on my own or run ahead out of excitement, the business tends to go sideways – which caused great fear on my part, especially when I watched my savings account dwindle!

When you are afraid, you give in to the anticipation of what could happen. We give fear such great power over us. Our imaginations are so strong that just the anticipation of an event causes our bodies to react in fight, flight, or freeze mode – even when nothing has actually happened yet. When you are fearful of something – real or imagined – you are tentative. You hesitate. You aren't sure what you should do. And as a leader, this can be very problematic!

People look to their leaders to see how they should react. If the leader is calm, then the people feel better. If the leader freaks out, so do the people! If the leader seems to have their head in the sand, then the people become fearful because they don't trust their leader to even know there *is* a problem.

You may have heard the acronym for fear: False Evidence Appearing Real. Fear holds so many people back from doing what they know they could do. So people settle instead of soar. They hunker down instead of jump up. They retreat instead of advance.

Franklin D. Roosevelt's first inaugural address as President of the United States was in 1933 and America was in the grip of the Great Depression. It is during this speech that he uttered those famous words, *"the only thing we have to fear is . . . fear itself — nameless, unreasoning, unjustified terror which paralyzes needed efforts to convert retreat into advance."*

Fear causes people to retreat.

Fearlessness, on the other hand, doesn't mean that you live without fear. Those people are a little bonkers. It's healthy to have a little fear. If we didn't, then the human race would have been wiped out a long time ago by sabre tooth tigers and more.

Instead, fearlessness is a knowingness that you will be ok. Fearlessness is not being afraid of what could happen. It is focused instead on opportunities. Fear is focused on what could go wrong. Fearlessness assumes things aren't wrong – just something to learn from. Thomas Edison, American inventor, said, *"I have not failed. I've just found 10,000 ways that won't work."* He was the epitome of when things went wrong, instead of wallowing in it, he learned from it and continued moving (or failing) forward.

I had a mentor tell me one time that God is pouring out His blessings on us like water gushing out of a fire hydrant. Most people are scared of the gush, so they stay on the sidelines and just get a little spray. They get some blessings, but not all that is available to them. I want to be swimming in the fabulous current of blessings!

Right now, how much would you say fear plays a part in your life and your decisions? How does it affect your leadership?

If you would like to commit to reducing your fear and increasing your fearlessness, here are eight steps you can do to aid in your success.

Give it up to God. Prayer is paramount.

Notice where fear shows up in your body. This can be a great trigger in recognizing fear is present. Is it showing up in pain in your stomach, in the tenseness of your neck, in the clenching of your hands? Notice where fear is showing up and write it down.

Make a list of your fears. Begin looking into what is causing your fear. What are some of your fears as a leader? By writing them down, you are taking some of the power away. Dig into the thoughts you hear when you see each fear on your list. It could be things such as, "if I make a wrong decision my team and my leadership won't respect or trust me anymore."

This week simply **notice when fear arises** in you and write it down. What fear showed up? What thoughts did you have around that fear? You don't have to do anything about it, but notice.

Ask – what's the worst thing that could happen if this fear comes true? Then ask, *then what?* Many times we get so caught up in the worst thing that could happen that we forget there is an afterwards. What will you do afterwards? Knowing you can come out on the other side can be a powerful fear reducer because you can make a plan to *do* something.

Ask – what are three gifts or benefits that could come from this situation? Sometimes it's not easy to answer while in the middle of it, but if you really try, then you begin to see the fear, the bad situation, as something more than what is or could be happening. This leads to learning from the situation which causes it not to be a failure but a learning instead.

Looking back at your list of fears, if one of those fears shows up, **ask yourself, what else could be true?** Sometimes your teenager not getting home in time for curfew is simply because they're kissing in the car. You don't have to go all the way to the fear that they crashed and are in the hospital or worse! What else could be true? What are the facts, not your assumptions? Begin to let a little of the fear go by questioning its veracity.

Create a plan of how you can get your fear under control. For most of us, when we are afraid our bodies go into stress mode –

meaning much of the oxygenated blood in our bodies run to our legs, our arms, and our chest to help us better fight or flee. But some of that oxygenated blood comes out of our brains, literally reducing our ability to think rationally. What plan do you have in place to increase the oxygen back to your brain? Deep breaths? Go for a walk? Think of that coral reef in Fiji (that's my go to!)?

Imagine if you were leading and you weren't afraid or worried about what your next decision is. You're focused on the outcome, on the journey, and you are fully in the moment, "in the flow."

What would it look like if you were to let some of your fears go?

How would you lead if you weren't afraid?

What is holding you back from being fearless?

What would change if you believed you had fearlessness?

What is your plan for being more fearless today?

You've written a list of your fears. Now on a new piece of paper, **write a list of what fearlessness looks like for you**. What are some beliefs or new rules you can implement to increase your fearlessness? Add those to your list. If you realize you're stepping back into fearfulness, what can you do to ease back to fearlessness? Add these to your list.

My fearlessness and my faithfulness have led to my company's success. My life is fun and I have met so many incredible people. I've been able to do what I do really well and learn so much more for my repertoire. I am joyful because I am fearless.

Have fearlessness in your life. With God at the head of your business, you have nothing to fear. Be fearless, be bold, be joyful.

To our success!

ABOUT SANDI MITCHELL

Sandi Mitchell is President of APEX Leadership Mastery, a firm dedicated to both people and profitability through intentional emphasis on emotionally intelligent leadership for extraordinary leaders. Her passion is working with high-achieving leaders who want to transition from leading followers to leading leaders.

APEX helps leaders build influence, confidence, and a coach-centric culture. We help leaders go from being a leader of followers to a leader of leaders.

APEX works with leaders from small businesses to major corporations to help improve and/or accelerate in areas such as: leadership presence and capability, senior team alignment, strategic planning, emotionally intelligent negotiations, and employee engagement. Her approach utilizes hands-on experiential learning, resulting in the highest impact and results through sustainable, long-term productivity improvements.

Sandi is certified as an executive coach who created and uses the APEX Leadership System™ – **A**wareness. **P**erformance. **E**xcellence. **X**traordinary. **L**eadership. She also specializes in emotionally intelligent negotiations through her EQ Negotiation™ program. Sandi is an international speaker and executive coach who connects to audiences, inspiring and motivating to reach even higher. She coaches exceptional people to be leaders AND leader makers.

For more information and to receive a free gift, please reach out to us at ApexMastery.com.

CONTACT SANDI MITCHELL

Sandi Mitchell
APEX Leadership Mastery
Awareness. **P**erformance. **E**xcellence. **X**traordinary. Leadership.

Phone: 682.200.1412
Email: Info@ApexMastery.com
Website: ApexMastery.com
LinkedIn: www.linkedin.com/in/sandimitchell
Facebook: https://www.facebook.com/sandi.mitchell.coaching
Twitter: @CoachSandiM

4. ESCAPING THE ENTREPRENEURIAL TRAP
BY BECKY LYNN SMITH

Every human being wages a personal battle to gain significance. We hunger for someone to validate our worth with some acknowledgement from the world that we exist – that we matter. We often seek significance in the wrong places. Some of us search for it in business. Others look for it in their job. Still others seek fame or to accumulate possessions.

My search for significance started at a young age and found its way into every aspect of my life. As an over achiever and people pleaser, I sought significance in the approval of other people and the world. I accumulated degrees, obtaining a BBA and MBA. I attained career success with an executive job title, a six-figure salary, bonus, company car, and corner office – all trappings of society's definition of success. But, when my stepsister who was my age died of a brain tumor, I stopped to evaluate the purpose and meaning of my life. I appeared to be successful, but deep down I did not feel that I was making a difference in the world. So I left my corporate job and bought a business coaching franchise.

As a business coach, I coached my clients on the need to create a balanced life. I spent most of my weekdays coaching and meeting with prospects. I spent weekends just trying to keep up with the other demands of my business. I had very little time for my family or myself. I was exhausted most of the time. That chaotic pace was not sustainable. I saw many of my clients struggling with these same issues.

The Entrepreneur's Trap

If the truth were known, many entrepreneurs get caught in this same trap. I was trying to do it all in my business. Even though I was attempting to do it all, much of it was falling through the cracks. I got caught in that chasm between having enough time to do it all and having enough money to pay someone else to do it. Many solo entrepreneurs never get over this gap. The gap prevents you from growing your business to a size that can support your family.

While I did love coaching, I found that I did not like chasing people for money. I despised sales. As a result, my business failed to generate enough revenue to survive. In denial, and trying to keep up the appearance of success, I drained my personal savings and racked up debt trying to stay afloat. The result - the business eventually failed, and I was left with the mountain of debt.

My search for significance was rooted in pride and ego. I wanted the world to validate my worth. Instead of seeking God's counsel about what I was to do to next, I projected the image that I had it all under control. All the while, I spent my time working harder while I was racking up more debt to create a picture of success for the world to view.

I think many of us fall into this trap. My mountain of debt is overwhelming evidence of the lengths to which my pride and ego would go to maintain the image of success. God has called me to help you understand that your significance is not found in the things of this world. It is not found in your title. It is not found in how many hours you work, or in recognition or awards or fame or fortune. **Your significance is found when you focus on God and love other people.**

Jesus replied:

" 'Love the Lord your God with all your heart and with all your soul and with all your mind.' This is the first and greatest commandment. And the second is like it: 'Love your neighbor as yourself.' All the Law and the Prophets hang on these two commandments." **Matthew 22:37-40 NIV**

Achieving significance requires you to spend quality time with God and with your family and friends. Unfortunately, many of us are just so busy chasing success that we run out of time for anything or anyone else. We get caught up in a never-ending spiral of busyness. God's plan for you includes more than enough time to do His work. His plan also includes making time for Him and your family.

We all need time to focus on God and on the people that matter the most. Jesus commanded that we love people. This most certainly includes your family and friends. The most important way to show your love for them is to give them your time. We as struggling entrepreneurs regularly sacrifice time with our families to build our businesses. We see it as a trade-off now for a payoff later. Later may never come. Tomorrow is promised to no one.

Balance is a struggle for all of us.

So many entrepreneurs I know are wired to be giving, but they don't make space for themselves, and then they don't have the bandwidth to help anyone else. - Yanik Silver

Balance is a struggle for all of us. We need time to stoke the fire – to find joy and strength to face life. We are all called to use our gifts and talents to serve God's purpose. God does not expect us to do more than we have time to do. And we are all given just enough time to do His will.

Entrepreneurs, your purpose – your reason for being – comes from Your Maker. He created your wiring, i.e., the unique blend of personality, behavior, talents, strengths, and values that make you uniquely you. God already knows the purpose for which He made you. Your plan for your life must align with God's plan to find success and balance.

If you find that you are running out of time or have too much to do, perhaps you need to evaluate what you are spending time on. Are your daily activities in alignment with God's purpose for your life? God's plan not only includes using your talents and gifts for His purpose, but His plan also includes time spent with Him and with your family and friends. This means that time, and not money, is your greatest asset. How are you spending your time?

"I command you to take a time out, Love, God."

The Bible provides the roadmap to show us how to live and do business God's way. How many of us regularly abuse the fourth commandment, *Remember the Sabbath day to keep it holy* **(Exodus 20:8 KJV)?"** I know I struggle with this one.

You may be thinking, yes, but I just don't have enough time to take a full day off for rest or to spend with my family. I am too busy. My inbox is full. I am struggling just to find time to make a living and to do everything that my business demands from me.

Even God, who is all-powerful, rested on the seventh day. Jesus regularly took time away from healing and teaching to rest and reflect. So why do we think we can be effective if we are working all of the time?

God did not strongly suggest you take a day off for rest. He *commanded* it. Now that must mean you are important to God. Are you REALLY doing business God's way?

God cares about us as human beings. He cared enough to command that you set aside a day to focus on the things that matter most in your life. The struggle is how do we balance the demands placed on us as entrepreneurs with the commandment that says we need to take 24 hours each week off?

God's plan includes a balanced life

We are all here to serve God with the talents and strengths He has given to us. And we all have different talents, but we all serve one purpose. That is God's purpose. I fully believe that you cannot have within you a desire to create a business in alignment with God's purpose without also at the same time having the capacity, natural abilities, and resources to bring it into reality. God would not give you a calling without also helping you find the time and provide the resources to get it done.

Consider for just a moment that perhaps God did not intend for you to do it all. After all, aren't there are other people in the world with a talent for doing those very things with which you struggle? Perhaps His plan includes engaging other people to help.

Until you, as a business owner, understand how your business fits within the calling that God has for your life, you will continue to struggle with time challenges.

It seems somewhat ironic, doesn't it? To find more balance out of the chaos, you must first find the time to focus on God and to reflect. To find more time, you must first take time out to focus on God. Ask Him how to bring your life into balance so that you can achieve the life of abundance he has planned for you. Balance is attainable, but only when your actions are in alignment with God's purpose for your life.

ABOUT BECKY LYNN SMITH

Becky Lynn Smith is an entrepreneur, author, and speaker on a mission to help solo entrepreneurs achieve greater success and balance in life.

Becky is the CEO of Coach Biz Solutions, Inc., and creator of eCoach360.com, the world's first fully integrated end-to-end coaching management platform. As the Director of Applications for a private Toyota distributor, Becky learned how to leverage people, process, and technology to achieve business results. As a business coach, Becky faced first-hand the struggle between not having enough money and not having enough time. The eCoach360 solution was created to help bridge this gap enabling coaches to focus on those things that matter most: **Love God and Love People** (Matthew 22: 37-39, paraphrased).

Becky holds a BBA, an MBA, and is working toward completion of a Doctor of Education degree in Organizational Leadership.

Becky's talents lie in helping other people get their stuff done. Along these lines she is a certified project management professional, DISC consultant, and behavioral life coach. Becky is the author of ***Designing Your Ideal Life*** and a contributor to Huffington Post and CNBC.com.

CONTACT BECKY LYNN SMITH

Entrepreneurs, how often do you take a good look at how your business is doing? Visit our website, and get your free business health checkup: http://ecoach360.com/free-offer.

Contact Links:

Email: becky@ecoach360.com

Phone: 713-412-8718

Websites: http://ecoach360.com and http://designingyourideallife.com

Facebook:

Like our Page at: https://www.facebook.com/spiritfedmindset

Visit Becky's personal page https://www.facebook.com/leadershipcoach.becky.smith and connect at: https://www.facebook.com/ecoach360 and https://www.facebook.com/DesigningYourIdealLife

Twitter: https://twitter.com/escapingsuccess

LinkedIn: https://www.linkedin.com/in/beckylynnsmith

5. JUST THE RIGHT ENOUGH
BY STEPHANIE SHERWOOD

I am going to start by telling you a story.

There once was a little girl who so desperately wanted to be heard, loved, and recognized for whom she was. It seemed every time she turned around someone was telling her "you are too much" - too dumb, too loud, too talkative, too squirmy, too nice, too hard to be around, too caring, too controlling, too much of a teacher's pet and the list goes on and on. Good or bad, she was too much.

The little girl wondered how she could have relationships and feel truly connected with people when she was always "too much." So she spent most of her life never really connecting, getting her feelings hurt, and trying super hard not to be "too much." She was exhausted trying to be "just right." Too much "bad" for some and then too much "good" for others.

After a while, she didn't know how to show up in life. She started to die a little bit every day, becoming numb. Never a smile, never a frown but oh how she mastered the art of the scowl, the art of not showing her emotions.

In her heart, she felt such a disconnect because she knew she was meant for more. It seemed like every time she turned around she kept running into the wall of "you are too much …" Too much good, too much bad. She became bitter and isolated because it hurt too much not to be liked and life simply didn't feel safe.

Despite those feelings, she tried to move forward because her heart yearned for more, even though she didn't know what "more" was. Repeatedly, she was told one way or another she was "too much" and her heart broke a little bit more each time.

The desire "to be more" returned to her and her heart. At first, it crept back in almost silently, only a bit at a time. But as the years went on and the cycle continued the desire "to be more" grew louder and louder and louder.

The little girl was now a woman, and she knew she was faced with the choice to continue to listen to "you are too much" or begin to listen to "be more." So she began to move toward what her heart was telling her to do, "to be more!"

And yes you guessed it, this story is about me. You may be wondering why I started my chapter in a book designed to reduce fear for the spirit-filled entrepreneur with a part of my childhood story. I have a simple answer. My story is about overcoming fear and recognizing the lies of the enemy, lies that I believed since I was at least five years old.

I have a very clear image of being at a family gathering, when I was around five, with one grandpa to my right and my other grandpa to my left. My little elbows perched on the table while my chin is resting gently in the palm of my hands. You see I was being paid a quarter not to talk. Because remember, I was "too much." I was excited because as a five-year-old little girl, I was with two of my favorite people, and I was the center of their attention. But what my grandpas meant for fun, the enemy took and twisted it around to make me play small. For at that moment, my value shifted, my value was attributed to not talking.

What I have come to learn over the decades is that God designed me with the gift to talk. Not to just talk about a few things, but to talk about a lot of things. Not to just talk about the easy things but to talk about the hard things. The things that go against culture, barriers, obstacles, and even the status quo.

My faith journey has been interesting too. My relationship with God started as a little girl. I felt safe knowing that He was there. Yet in my little girl brain, I had envisioned the Trinity as linear. God first, then Jesus and the Holy Spirit. To be honest, I didn't fully grasp the truth of the Trinity until about five years ago. You may not think that is a big deal but what you may not know is that five years ago I started the Tapestry Network, an organization that supports and encourages Christian businesswomen and seekers to grow in faith and business.

Yup, that's right, a woman who didn't even truly understand the Trinity was called to start a business to support Christian businesswomen. God most definitely has a sense of humor. It wasn't until I had been running the business for about a year that I came to fully grasp that I had the same Holy Spirit that raised Jesus Christ from the dead inside of me. That I could call on Him whenever I needed Him to be with me, to guide me, to help me, to love me, and to teach me. I also need to share that I didn't have my first truly intimate experience with Jesus until the spring of 2015. Yes, I know that my story is ironic. But isn't that the way God works? He takes the things that don't make sense and when we are willing to be open and to share He makes our stories beautiful.

To be honest, at first, it was hard to share my lack of understanding on something that is so fundamental about the Bible. Even now there are times where I will begin to wince at the order that things have happened for me. But if I stayed in that spot of fear and doubt of what people might think of me I would slide back into; "See? You are 'too dumb.'" But my story isn't about me. My story is about God. It's a story about how God can use anyone for anything when there is a willing heart. When I stand above my fear God is glorified and my story brings Kingdom impact. You see it really isn't the order of things or the story itself; it is what you choose to do with it that truly matters!

In 2009, I hit my personal rock bottom after my husband found out about a $30,000 secret I had kept from him. I was trying to keep my business afloat with credit cards and as the economy began to sink it caught up with me. I am blessed to say that we are still married, and our relationship has never been better. But what you also need to know is my husband isn't yet a believer. There are times where I sit back and think, "Why has my marriage been spared when so many others haven't been?" It is in those moments of stinkin' thinkin' that we allow the enemy to take a foot hold. What we need to do is meditate on Isaiah 55:8-9. It says:

"My thoughts are nothing like your thoughts," says the LORD. "And my ways are far beyond anything you could imagine. ⁹ For just as the heavens are higher than the earth, so my ways are higher than your ways and my thoughts higher than your thoughts."

It is not for me to figure out; however, it is for me to share about God's mercy and grace. It is for me to take every opportunity to share where my life story might glorify Him. If I don't, then I keep my focus on me and not where it belongs, on Him!

They often say what makes you mad, what brings you to tears and what pisses you off is where you will probably find your calling. It was after my secret was discovered that I recommitted myself to the Lord, and the journey to my calling started to be revealed. Soon after I recommitted myself, I signed up for my first women's Bible study. I was so excited to get to know other like-minded women that I could relate to. My Bible study journey began in a mega church with over 1,200 women in attendance. We met on Tuesday night and 98% of the women there were in the workforce as employees, employers, entrepreneurs and small business owners. My heart was full as I was so excited to not only have the like-mindedness of women seeking a more personal relationship with God but the like-mindedness of women who were also in the marketplace.

What I learned very quickly is that talking about anything to do with work was only acceptable if a woman was out of work. But I had issues. I had questions. I had concerns that I wanted to seek answers to, from women who were like me – Christian businesswomen in the marketplace. I also learned just as quickly it was okay to talk about kids, husbands, and illnesses. Why was this?

At Bible study, I could talk about how I was falling in love with Jesus, but I couldn't have that conversation in the marketplace. At church, I couldn't talk or share about issues or concerns around my job. I began to see how my "to be more" was showing up. God had strategically placed me in the marketplace, and I began to get frustrated. Really frustrated. My thought process was, "I don't think God has designed me to live two separate lives." God is about completeness and the place I was in was making me feel anything but complete.

I was beginning to get so many mixed messages about what was acceptable for a Christian woman. There are so many stories in the Bible where women have stepped out and have had a tremendous impact for God. They have gone against the culture, the status quo and have overcome huge barriers and obstacles. Yet, as a church, these are the stories that often aren't shared, discussed or studied. I was beginning to feel as if I had no value to the church for you see, "I was too much." The church seemed to be okay with women that had "traditional roles." These women were the stay-at-home moms or women that held conventional jobs; teachers, nurses, administrative positions, etc. But what about me? Why didn't I count? Why didn't I have value? And what started to boil in my heart was that I needed to be all that God had called me to be without apology! I went to my Bible for direction and what I found was *Colossians 3:23-24 (AMP).*

"Whatever you do [whatever your task may be], work from the soul [that is, put in your very best effort], as [something done] for the Lord and not for men, [24] knowing [with all certainty] that it is from the Lord [not from men] that you will receive the inheritance which is your [greatest] reward. It is the Lord Christ whom you [actually] serve."

My responsibility was to serve Jesus – period!

As I began to pray and seek what He had for me, He began to show me that I, like everyone else who believes, had a calling that only I could do. He designed me before the beginning of time. He knows every hair on my head, and He knows my heart. He has to; because that is what His word says and He is incapable of anything but truth! My calling was to take my gift to talk and begin to use my voice to speak truth. The truth that women matter, the truth that women can have a voice, the truth about the new covenant, the truth about the history of the Bible, the truth that many have taken God's word and manipulated it to serve their purpose, especially to keep women small. My truth is to expand the voice of God and silence the voice of the enemy!

In my calling, I have been directed to create a community, a business. This business has created a space where women can get fed, can be a part of something bigger than themselves, can find healing and acceptance right where they are, without judgment. They get to see, experience and feel the love of Jesus. They get to stand in their greatness and be all that God has called them to be without apology! Along the way, God has taught us a thing or two.

1. **We can have the same gifts and still be in community together!**
   If we take the way of the world, our goal would be to take our competitor out. God isn't glorified in this. When we remember we serve an abundant God, we realize He does not set-up one of us for success and the other for failure. With this truth and perspective, we can come alongside our sisters-in-business and support one another

in life and business. God is glorified in this! **Ephesians 3:20**

2. **The world's idea of success cannot be our idea of success!**

   As business people, the world tells us what matters most is the transaction and the money it puts in our bank accounts. Yet as believers we have two bank accounts: our temporal account (green stuff in the bank) and our eternal bank account (our treasures stored in heaven). Our eternal bank account is measured not by transaction but by the value of what we bring to the exchange. When our focus is on our eternal bank account, then we are keeping our eyes on Jesus and not ourselves. **Matthew 6:19-21**

3. **Our comfort is not His primary concern!**

   The world tells us to keep our skeletons in the closet. We are much better off walking around with the necklaces of shame, lies and fears around our necks. No healing, no transformation, no growth, no change comes from this. The world's thinking keeps us stuck and in despair. God knows that healing comes in sharing and true community. Sharing is uncomfortable, but sharing takes our eyes off us and puts them on Him. Sharing and truth bring freedom. **Isiah 61:1-3 | Romans 12:2**

My challenge to you is to find a community where you can be the "real you." The YOU God created you to be without apology. The YOU that He designed for greatness; that YOU is on the earth right now because there is something that God needs and only YOU can do it. Whether The Tapestry Network or somewhere else – find your community and be your version of "just the right enough" for His glory!

ABOUT STEPHANIE SHERWOOD

Stephanie simply is a woman who loves to serve. As a child it was taking dessert orders at family parties and listening to her friends to help them work through their problems. As an adult not much has changed!

In addition to 18 years in Corporate America, Stephanie has been a full-fledged entrepreneur for well-over a decade. Taking the same core skills from her childhood of service and problem solving, Stephanie spent most of her corporate career rebuilding and growing award winning teams. Stephanie has always rallied for change to better serve the needs of employees and clients. However, her biggest accomplishments are always focused on lifting others up, whether that was helping someone to find their courage to pursue their dream or building her own company so she could hire women and lift them up. Those are her true successes.

Along the way Stephanie has found a void in the marketplace

where Christian businesswomen can show-up and be all that God has designed and called them to be without apology. After making a bold statement to God about wanting to serve and advance His kingdom, Stephanie was gifted with many visions that have led her to The Tapestry Network as a Founder/CEO. As Founder/CEO, Stephanie's vision is to expand the voice of God and to silence the voice of the enemy.

Stephanie lives in Northern California with her husband of almost 30 years. They have two children and were just blessed with two grandchildren.

CONTACT STEPHANIE SHERWOOD

Websites:

www.thetapestrynetwork.com

www.stephaniesherwoodtalks.com

www.1thingbooks.com

Connect on social media:

www.facebook.com/StephanieMorinSherwood

www.facebook.com/TheTapestryNetwork

www.twitter.com/TapestryNet

www.pinterest.com/TapestryNet

www.linkedin.com/in/sherwoodstephanie

Email: stephanie@thetapestrynetwork.com

Phone: 916.521.2540

Sign-up for a FREE 30-Day trail on-line Tapestry Network membership and a FREE REPORT "Ten Networking

Secrets that Will Grow Your Business" and get "Tapped In"!!!
www.thetapestrynetwork.com/join/online-membership/

6. SPIRIT MINDSET: ABSOLUTE FREEDOM
BY CHRISTINE GILARDI M.ED.

Absolute freedom is having complete certainty that one can receive a reliable answer to any given question for the most beneficial outcome. We are positioned to achieve absolute freedom when we are completely aligned with our conscious mind, our intuition, and the wisdom expressed through our bodies' electromagnetic frequencies. In this state, we can easily discern whether the answer to any question is a "yes" or a "no;" in some cases, the energy is not yet determined and "no answer" is the answer. Absolute freedom comes through this process of becoming an astute, intuitive practitioner, a steward of the inner world.

To grow a business, or even just live with a fearless mindset, we must become a steward of our inner world—we must constantly deepen our grounding in faith and get very clear about our beliefs. We re-evaluate where we put our faith, and we let go of old beliefs that are no longer working in our lives. We surround ourselves with others who fully support us; we let go of relationships that are complete. We forgive the past, ourselves, and others--clearing out the old to make room for the new.

Developing intuitive sensitivity is a process that comes more easily for some than others. We must practice to expand our intuitive connection with our higher self and interpret signals within our physical body, through its ability to express with a variety of sensations.

INTUITION 101: Absolute freedom is "complete knowing" what to do in any given situation; turning within and receiving guidance is instantaneous and 100% accurate.

What does a "yes" feel like?

Has someone told you a story, and you immediately got the chills, head to toe? Little hairs on your arm stood up tingling? You knew it was TRUE. That is your body's electromagnetic charge for a "yes" impulse. Think of a lie detector test. Your body's innate wisdom NEVER lies.

What does a "no" feel like?

Has someone told you a lie and you immediately got this uncomfortable feeling in your gut, your solar plexus? The body's wisdom is expressed, and the knowingness is instantaneous. There is no decision-making process, pondering, considering, rationalizing, comparing, contrasting, waiting, confusion, anxiety... just a simple answer in real time. This is absolute freedom. Knowing what to do next negates fear.

The seasoned intuitive practitioner develops the awareness that NO ONE can deny. The experience of "TRUTH" is an internal one, and there is no getting around the certainty of the physical feeling when our bodies give us answers. This is absolute freedom.

What about the ego and negative chatter? Can I really trust the answers from within? Scientific data purports that the average human being has about 25,000 to 50,000 thoughts a day—what is the preponderance of your thoughts . . . about your business? Your life? Researchers in psychology have linked depression with negative thought patterns. How does anyone escape?

We escape as we develop astute awareness—moment to moment— by staying tuned into what we are thinking. If/when we hear a thought that we do not like, we cancel it. Replace it. We learn to be vigilant with our thoughts as they are the seeds in the garden of authentic freedom; we learn to be the Master of our Ship, the Captain of our Destiny.

We understand how to be sensitive to the tone that comes from within. If the inner voice sounds like a victim, that's a sign that the ego is crying out for attention. Victim thoughts are diminishing, *"Who are you to do this? Who cares what you have to say?"* We, as humans, can experience a pattern of negative thinking that can literally suck the life force out of us. Developing the ability to listen to "who" is speaking as the voice from within, and if the victim shows up, self-parent, self-talk. *"I know you feel that way, but since everything works out, you really are not a victim, are you?"* Humor is a great tool to disarm the ego. Past pain must be identified and resolved.

What do my life and my business look like when I am completely free?

To understand absolute freedom, let us review its polar opposite, paralyzing, gripping, crippling fear. Fear is the "fight-or-flight" response, which is an innate survival instinct in human beings. In our early human history, when danger was lurking around every corner and we had to kill to eat (or in some cases, kill or be killed), this response was lifesaving. However, in our modern times, it is rare that we are faced with deadly situations.

CASE STORY-Agoraphobia: Few human experiences are as isolating and painful as agoraphobia: living in the grips of panic attacks, the truly perceiving danger is present, even when the logical mind knows nothing harmful is happening. The sensations in panic attacks, as in other anxiety disorders, are indicators that the innate "fight or flight" response is activated, adrenaline rushing, quickening our breath, heightening our senses, readying us for escape from impending danger. The agoraphobic, believing that the situation is terrifying and imminently harmful, is overwhelmed and paralyzed. This process leads to extreme isolation, which alone can be the cause of additional pain since the human spirit was made for interaction and community.

I had a client named Mary, who had been unable to leave her home for many years. She described it as feeling completely terrified to leave home for any reason. She was dependent on her husband for everything. Mary had gone to many doctors for help, but up until this point, no one had been able to help her.

After one 30-minute call, in which we were able to activate her inner knowing of her power and her infinite Spirit, she was immediately transformed. I met her husband some years later, and he told me that the work we did that day was a miracle; he said they "even go to the beach." What changed? Why was the shift possible in a matter of minutes when the symptom had been present for many years?

Spirit is not bound by space nor time, which are human constructs. Spirit is truly infinite, omniscient, omnipresent, and immortal. We are Divine Spirits in Human Bodies having opportunities to deepen our sense of who we are and the impact we can have as beings on Earth, each one part of a whole, the Divine consciousness. Mary needed to be reminded WHO she IS. Mary's story can be an analogy for us. In what ways are we "stuck at home?" In what areas of our businesses are we living in fear, terrified, paralyzed?

Scripture is clear that we must ask to receive; we must take action to move forward. During the Sermon on the Mount Jesus said,

> *"⁷Ask and it will be given to you; seek and you will find; knock and the door will be opened to you. ⁸ For everyone who asks receives; the one who seeks finds; and to the one who knocks, the door will be opened."* (Matthew 7:7–8).

Intuition is a most powerful vehicle for asking and receiving; it is a demonstration of Divine Laws and Jesus' teaching "The Kingdom is Within."

Much like in our personal lives, our businesses prosper, and blessings flow when we are centered in the here and now, at peace, living our Truth, our Purpose, and our Mission. As we refine our intuitive skills, we receive guidance for the next action steps, one step at a time. Intuition is God's gift to us—it is one of the greatest gifts—it is the vehicle through which we can truly live authentically—fearlessly.

Growing a business with a fearless mindset requires the awareness and inner conviction that by its very nature, this business is blessed; that its existence is serving others, and therefore, it is further blessed; that I am expanding my abilities and skills to be a better leader and servant, and therefore, it is further blessed; that I am expanding my reach and the positive impact I can have on others, and therefore, it is further blessed; and I am perfectly positioned to help empower others, and therefore, it is further blessed, etc.

Framing life as an opportunity and a blessing [and not a burden (ego/victim)] is a critical rite of passage into Spiritual maturity. Since we are infinite Spirits, every impress that comes to us is a Divine Communication . . .

of Possibility . . .

Potentiality . . .

Transformation . . .

Evolution.

The best of us as Humans comes from our nature as Spiritual Beings.

Human Experience + Awareness of Spiritual Nature = Heaven on Earth

If absolute fear is a human experience, then absolute freedom is the Truth of Spirit. When we choose a spiritual path, we can mitigate human fear with the power of our spiritual essence and live life to our fullest potential. Our awakened Spirit in human form defines Heaven on Earth.

ABOUT CHRISTINE GILARDI M.Ed.

Gilardi gained national acclaim in the 2013 Posi-Fest Awards with Honorable Mention for "I Believe in Love," a song that she wrote for Melissa Etheridge. Gilardi's straight-ahead rock and blues arrangements, infused with positive messages, are common threads. She is an improvisational songwriter, an Open Mic Host, and a featured blues jam performer at Boogie Jams, SD Jamming Out at the House of Blues, and other area venues. JAMMINGOUT   VIDEO: https://www.youtube.com/watch?v=cFQgUcZpOf8

In 2014, Gilardi teamed up with award winning singer-songwriter Lacy Younger and they performed at the 2014 Temecula International Film & Music Festival, as one of only 10 acts selected from thousands. In 2015, she was 1 of 5 finalists in the 2015 NM Music Awards in the vocal performance category for her hit single, "I Miss You," produced by Grammy Award Winning Artist/Producer Larry Mitchell. In 2016, Gilardi is building a new SD Chapter of the Women's Global Leadership Alliance (WGLA) to unite female musicians, artists and entrepreneurs for leadership opportunities and local, regional, national, and international collaboration. Gilardi is a gifted intuitive coach and mentor, committed to help others achieve their dreams.

After spending years healing and shedding over 130 pounds, Gilardi's personal story has swept through the SD music scene, bringing love and inspiration to her peers and fans alike. MY TRANSFORMATION   VIDEO-YouTube https://www.youtube.com/watch?v=-RXUshMxCYE

CONTACT CHRISTINE GILARDI M.Ed.

Gilardi has 3 albums for sale as well as her hit single "I Miss You" at her web site www.MamaChristy.com

Email: ChristineGilardi@mac.com

Web Site: www.MamaChristy.com, www.ChristineGilardi.com (coming soon)

Facebook: https://www.facebook.com/christinegilardi

Twitter: https://twitter.com/mamachristy

Facebook Artist Page:
https://www.facebook.com/MamaChristy336

LinkedIn: https://www.linkedin.com/in/christygilardi

Play Like a Girl Records Artist:
http://playlikeagirlrecords.com/artists/christine-gilardi/

Director, SD Chapter WGLA:
http://womensgla.com/?affiliates=29

7. LIVING LIFE THROUGH THE LENS OF IMPROV
BY CLAIRE BILLINGSLEY

Many of you have seen the show on TV called "Whose Line Is It Anyway?" or, perhaps you have had the chance to actually see an improv troupe performance. If so, you know that improv is much different from stand-up comedy, as, in improv, there is nothing scripted. Stand-up comedians get the chance to practice their scripts, timing, facial expressions, etc. before they go on stage. And the next show you see will probably be very similar one night to the next.

It's not sketch comedy either like you see on "Saturday Night Live." Even though there may be a bit of true improv sprinkled in, the vast majority of their work is written material that the actors perform. In true improv, it is totally made-up-on-the-spot entertainment, based on suggestions the Director gets from the crowd.

Improv could be called "high-risk creative work." Not only do we have to keep our egos in check to be openly collaborative, but we always keep in mind we are there for the audience. And their expectation is that we are to please them consistently. We are on stage, thinking on our feet in front of the audience, basically "writing" our "sketch" one line at a time in front of the audience, where there is no time for rewrites. It's all there for your viewing pleasure. There are rules that we follow, and that is what we rehearse every week, learning the rules stone cold, so they are like muscle memory in our mind. This way, when we have all the other distractions around us on stage, we are still able to focus on each other and to make our partners look brilliant.

Since we don't know what the suggestion is going to be until we hear it, it is imperative that we all trust each other and have each other's back. This is a foundational building block that all great improvisers embrace and emphatically follow.

In improv, we have two concurrent things on our minds constantly – actively listening to our scene partner's ideas and then adding our own ideas to move the scene forward. The exchange and adaptation to the constant change of the direction of the scene is the main goal for us as we create together. These are just two foundational "rules" that we follow to help us take care of each other.

As I began to really evaluate the improvisational comedy "code of conduct", or "rules", I realized that all of them dovetailed beautifully into the business world. And what about just having plain old fun at work? Since when has that been given a bad rap?

It is this curiosity that sprang from those questions I asked myself several years ago that my shift in how I approach life occurred. I went from feeling like I didn't fit in anywhere, to a place where I was not just ok, but celebrated. It wasn't about how pretty you were or how much money you made every year, it was about a "status free" environment where everyone was treated equal. Yes, we played characters that have more status than the other, such as Captain and a Sailor; but off the stage, everyone was treated the same. Everyone's contributions mattered. And we always assumed the best of each other. That was a place I could really get excited about!

My background isn't in the theater, although I was quite the master of morphing into something I wasn't at my core for many years in the business world. I spent 25 years trying to fit into the corporate America role. I was told I was "too nice." I was told I "laughed too loud." And that I "thanked people too much." I got "too wrapped up in how other people were feeling." I tried to change – I really did – and was pretty successful in my work along the way. I won awards, I got promoted, I was transferred to work on bigger projects or new companies, but it was always an act. One that was incredibly stressful. It takes a lot of energy to show up as a person who is not authentic and aligned with your core beliefs. And I think a lot of people put that same mask on every day that I did for so long because they are told that is what they need to do to survive in the environment.

When I tell people I use improvisational comedy to open up lines of communication for groups and organizations; their eyes light up. "Really? How fun!" they say. And it makes me kind of sad because they have no idea how it feels to be happy at what you do. There's a song from the "80's called "WHAM Rap" – yes, WHAM wrote a rap song. The line from that song that has always stuck with me is "do you enjoy what you do . . . if not, just stop, don't stay there and rot." Yet, so many of us do that every day. We are stuck in a place that does not support our values, our vision, our culture, our work ethic, or our creativity. But we go in every day, like zombies, put in our time, and then leave. Like another '80's band, Loverboy said, "Everybody's working for the weekend."

We all want and need to feel good. It is one of those very basic human needs. The desire to feel good, to change a mood, or even loosen up a bit, is the reason many people turn to alcohol or even legal and illegal drugs. However, there is no way that any man-made substance can be as powerful as the endorphins that the body produces for free, without any side-effects.

Laughter releases endorphins that are more powerful than morphine. These endorphins can lead to a sense of well-being and optimism. In addition, humor and laughter can bridge the gap between total strangers. The use of humor can even reduce tension in a tense situation (as workplaces can sometimes be). Have you ever been in a comedy house and listened to the laughter? One person may start, and then the laughter grows as more and more people "get" the joke or see that they too have permission to have fun in the moment. Have you ever looked at someone at another table in a comedy house, made eye contact, and laughed at the same time, even though you didn't know them? You were actually transferring positive energy from one person to another. Or you had a great coffee chat with an old friend? You feel so light and almost giddy when you leave each other. Those moments are created by the feeling of being "in" on the same joke, or experiences, which creates a common bond.

These small moments can also be generated in the workplace. You can have a mood of geniality and support and creativity by creating mutual experiences and opportunities for success with your teams . . . or you can have a mood of resentment, fear, and despair. What type of mood do you project to your employees every day? Which mood will bring you more productivity from your team?

The good news is, there is a choice on how you choose to show up each day. You have a choice of modeling what good looks like for your organization. You get the honor of setting the "stage" to set your "performers" up for success! How? By delivering lines that help them see clearly what you are looking for in their performance that day. Give your team clear and decisive direction. Aren't you excited?

Henri Poincare said, "It is through science that we prove, but through intuition that we discover." So much of improv is instinct. You almost have to let your subconscious take over and trust it will guide you. In that light, it is similar to spirituality, because you really don't know where you are going, and how you are going to get there, but you trust in the people on stage with you . . . and you trust in the process. The decision you make in improv is never wrong. Sure, there are higher percentage choices you can make, but at the end of the day, you reflect back and think about the choices you made, the outcomes they produced, and then determine if you liked the way it turned out. Maybe next time you change it. So, you have no reason just to go for it and see what happens.

From the 14 years I have been involved in improvisational comedy, I have learned that me showing up authentically is the best gift I can give myself and everyone else in the world. So how about you? There is only one you. You were created for a reason. Be yourself. As Dr. Seuss says "Why blend in when you were created to stand out?"

Be your awesome self. I grant you permission.

ABOUT CLAIRE BILLINGSLEY

Billingsley Consulting Group is a training and communications firm designed to help businesses, associations, and educational institutions grow through personal and professional development. Claire Billingsley has experience coaching managers on social and communication skills, leadership skills, time management and organizational skills, personnel management, as well as personal and professional development. Claire held leadership and management positions with Sylvan Learning Systems, FASTSIGNS International, and TONI&GUY Hairdressing Academy. With over 20 years of business experience, she learned the strategies and skills necessary to lead, manage, and motivate employees spread all over the world. Claire is a graduate of Emporia State University, a Certified Franchise Executive through the International Franchise Association and a trained executive Ontological business coach. She is a mentor and former Chairman of the Board at The University of North Texas Professional Leadership Program, College of Business.

Calling on her background in Improvisational comedy, Claire's workshops use participatory-style training methods that teach practical knowledge and skills through highly interactive methodologies and real life business lessons. Claire's workshops take the skills and guiding principles taught through improvisational comedy and demonstrates how they transfer to the workplace. Her techniques help individuals and organizations foster innovation, build confidence, take initiative, improve communication skills, collaborate, take risks and enhance creativity.

In 2010, Claire was named one of the "Top 25 Women to Watch" in Dallas by the Dallas Business Journal.

Claire is the author of "Circle Up!" – available on Amazon.com, and is a certified Laughter Yoga Leader.

CONTACT CLAIRE BILLINGSLEY

Website: www.billingsleyconsultinggroup.com
Twitter: ImprovBizClaire
LinkedIn: Claire Billingsley
Facebook: Claire Billingsley and Laughter Yoga/WINE Down Yoga
You Tube: Claire Billingsley
Cell Phone: 214.289.8802
Best emails:
Claire@Billingsleyconsultinggroup.com or Billingsley.Consulting @gmail.com

8. LIES WE BELIEVE ABOUT FEAR
BY CATHRYN CLARKSON-FINLEY

"So do not fear, for I am with you; do not be dismayed, for I am your God. I will strengthen you and help you; I will uphold you with my righteous right hand." Isaiah 41:10

His words are "life" words, soothing to our soul, calming to our spirits, giving power to our days.

If we love God and are following the commands of Jesus and if you are a believer, the Bible says all things work together for your good and the Glory of God. (Romans 8:28) There is no difficulty, dilemma, defeat, disaster or FEAR in the life of a believer that God can't ultimately get some good out of, so what is there to FEAR?

Most of what I have learned over the years about FEAR is not true.

- Fear is not False Evidence Appearing Real
- Fear is not Failure Expected and Received
- Fear is not Face Evidence and Rejoice
- Fear is not Forget Everything and Relax
- Fear does not go away after reading positive Affirmations with positive thinking.

"The Lord is with me; I will not be afraid. What can man do to me? The Lord is with me; he is my helper." Psalm 118:6-7

What Can Man Do to Me?

Rejection, worry, procrastination, clutter, envy, unbelief, anxiety, I could go on and on. Every single one of these thoughts and feelings is driven by fear. The most persistent fear I have repeatedly overcome personally and professionally is fear of rejection. I refer to this fear as the people pleasing fear because it

48

can manifest into other fears. A people pleaser is one comparing yourself to other people, telling yourself that it might not work, afraid of what other people will think or say about you, not confident about what you know, wondering if anyone will value what you have to say. Can I get a witness? Have you ever felt this way before?

When I was 18 years old, if only I had known what I now know. Don't worry if people don't like you. Most people are struggling to like themselves. I didn't know what this emotional feeling was, but I always had the need to prove myself. I wanted to feel important, validated and loved. I cared so much about pleasing everybody else and didn't care enough about myself.

I thought that if I could get everyone to like me or accept me this deep fear of feeling rejected and needing to be recognized would fade, and I would be happy. Time passed and much to my surprise I found out that I could never win the approval of everyone, so I found a way to embrace rejection. It was a long time before I found out this wasn't the answer and my hard work was still in front of me. There is one area that will make or break all of your hard work as it relates to fear. This area is your **MINDSET**, let's call this a **MINDSET SHIFT** and I will be coming back to this a little later in my chapter.

"I prayed to the Lord, and he answered me. He freed me from all my fears." Psalm 34:4

Something Missing

The most pivotal moment of my life happened in January 1982. After 20 years of marriage and three children, I found myself divorced. In my mind, at the time, divorce was the ultimate rejection. At night when the boys were asleep, I felt alone. The only positive I found in being alone is because this is where moments of inspiration unfold. Isolation and rejection can steal your joy. I was passionate and purposeful raising my sons, but in my professional work something was missing.

On my journey, it was one connection that was constant and HE transformed my life.

The Lord is my light and my salvation—whom shall I fear? The Lord is the stronghold of my life—of whom shall I be afraid?" Psalm 27:1

One Sunday sitting in a church service and hearing the Gospel of Jesus I wept like never before. The weight of my sin and brokenness of fear, rejection, worry, and all of those other lies lifted off my shoulder. It wasn't an Aha moment or even a light bulb moment, it was a *"Hallelujah!", "Thank you Jesus!"* moment. Even after my *"Hallelujah, thank you Jesus!"* moment, I still struggled with identity issues, sadness and feeling inadequate from time to time. But now these fears point me to the cross. The most beautiful thing is that in our weakness, God's strength is displayed perfectly. To prove my point God was not through with me yet.

Personally, I had made the connection with God, but as it relates to my professional speaking career and business in general, I still had some work to do. Everything in life is more meaningful when you make connection with God your goal. I was not alone. Jesus is the only way to heal; he makes all things new.

After ending a sales and marketing career, where you didn't dare talk about God or your faith, I automatically transferred that lesson to my new world of Public Speaking and onto my stage. When I spoke, that was something that was missing and I knew it. It was the most important part of my life, my faith in God and who I had become as a Christian.

When I started my speaking career 23 years ago, I was fearful I might be rejected if I talked about my faith on stage. As a public speaker, I was cautious when it came to integrating God into my business especially my speeches from the stage.

A Well-Kept Secret

Over the years, I have spoken on many stages here in the United States and internationally to individuals from all walks of life. I kept my faith a secret from my audience. That was the only way because at the time it was not being done and in my mind, I felt it was not acceptable in the industry. As I look back over that time in my life, I must confess that no one ever told me to leave my faith out of my speeches.

A few years later I joined a group of entrepreneurs and invested in a company with other Personal Development Coaches. The name of the company was The Peoples Network. I was able to attend seminars with the likes of Jeff Olsen, Eric Worre, Jim Rohn, Les Brown, Mark Victor Hanson, to name a few. If I had not been a part of this company, I would have to pay thousands of dollars to attend their seminars. At the time, I didn't know it, but this was a gift from God.

One evening I sat listening to this speaker, and if I called his name, you would know exactly who I am talking about. He talks about "you've got to be hungry" in his speeches. I will never forget the moment he was sharing his personal story, and he integrated God and Scripture into his speech. I wanted to stand up and start screaming *"Praise The Lord!", "Praise The Lord!".* Did he just say God and quote scripture? Now I didn't know anything about his faith. Then I realized he could speak about his faith without preaching. God had just opened up the windows and poured out a blessing because I had never heard a speaker talk about their faith from the stage before.

"He will give you the desires of your heart and not the spirit of fear." Psalm 37:4

I began to really listen to other motivational speakers and much to my surprise I began to hear other speakers talk about their faith in God in their speeches. I said to myself I've got this; I could do this too. My spirit overflowed with joy and happiness as if a heavy burden lifted. I was inspired, but it took hearing other speakers from stage speak their faith outside the church before I believed I could do the same. I made up my mind from now on I was ready to get rid of the fear and speak my faith. It made a tremendous difference in my presentations. Today I am free to speak and share my God-given gifts with my audience. It feels so good to be free to be real. No secrets. No lies. No hiding my faith. As a result of being obedient, he has given me the desires of my heart.

We Fear Only What We Don't Understand.

I mentioned earlier in this chapter about hard work, and this one area will make or break all of your hard work and that's having a **MINDSET SHIFT**. Every single one of the thoughts and feelings I discussed in this chapter is driven by fear.

Your mindset is something you can shift if you are dedicated to understanding why you feel a certain way at any given time, and also be willing to do the work. It's hard work, and it's a process. Let me be real and let's face the facts.

Fear isn't going anywhere. However, we do have the opportunity to change our mindset. We can change how we react to fear so that it's no longer something we allow to hold us back.

"Even though I walk through the valley of the shadow of death, I will fear no evil, for you are with me; your rod and your staff, they comfort me." Psalm 23:4

FEAR Is but A Shadow

Jesus walks with us through our valleys. He may not deliver us out of the valley, but He most certainly does not abandon us in the valley. Our fear many times, is but a shadow of Satan. It is not real. It seems like reality, but it is not. It is but a reflection of the evil one. So we have no need to fear because of our Heavenly Father bright light of love.

When I look at fear today and talk about breaking through fear, I'm not saying that I don't or won't still feel those feelings. Now I am able and you can too take your FEARS to the LORD in prayer. He will bring clarity to your confusion. Saturate your soul with truth, and you will flush out your fear. HE became the one I value most and HE makes sure that all of our needs are met. Today more than ever I trust Him as I face my fears, whether personally or professionally, death or life. Trust in Christ is a bridge to your fear, above all else, trust in the LORD overcomes fear.

Then He who sat on the throne said, "Behold, I make all things new." And He said to me, "Write, for these words are true and faithful."- Revelation 21:5

Father in heaven, thank You for every new day. Thank You for the opportunity to begin again. I choose to press forward and keep believing for the dreams and desires, not the fears, You've placed in my heart. I trust You today with everything that I am in Jesus' name. Amen

Start Living Your Life *FEARLESSLY!*

ABOUT CATHRYN CLARKSON-FINLEY

A native of Dallas, Texas Cathryn Clarkson Finley is a speaker, author, spiritual advisor, she carries a ministry inside of her spirit that encourages and support women in every stage of life. As a domestic violence advocate, she has a burning desire in her heart to help women who have been abused mentally or physically. After traveling throughout the United States and Internationally as a Product Education Trainer and Product Developer for Artistry Cosmetics within a billion-dollar marketing company and for the Mortgage Industry as a Contract Mortgage Underwriter she subsequently began her network marketing career on a part time basis.

Today Cathryn is a full time Senior Director with Stream Home Life Services, marketing deregulated energy, wireless and other life essential services that everyone uses. Stream Services fit into everyone's budget, people are already paying for them every single month and she is empowered helping other people succeed while building a passive residual income that you can depend on. She and her husband Melvin Finley Jr are the proud Recipients of the Stream 2013 Power of Leadership Award. This award is given annually to 30 Stream Associates from their over 300,000 Associates for outstanding leadership helping other's succeed while giving people the tools to become self-sufficient professionally and in business.

Cathryn became an International Best Selling Author in 2013 a collaboration with 29 other Authors who all have unique experience when it comes to networking. Title of her Best Selling Book is Network to Increase Your Net Worth. Their enthusiasm is contagious and their message of what it takes to succeed not only in business but also in life is a message about making good choices and never giving up.

Her greatest Blessing and Joy is that of being a wife to Melvin, for over 30 years, mom to 3 adult sons, together she and her husband share 5 children, 7 grandchildren and they make their home in Desoto, Texas. Cathyn's favorite quote is **"Everything you want is right outside your comfort zone"**!

CONTACT CATHRYN CLARKSON-FINLEY

Free Offer: www.mfinley.mystream.com you could be earning free credits on your mobile and energy bill in three simple steps. Energy Free

Email: finley3and10@gmail.com

Phone: 972-47-0068

Website: www.mfinley.mystream.com

Facebook: http://www.facebook.com/cathrynfinley

Pinterest: http://pinterest.com/cfinley180

Email: finley3and10@gmail.com

LinkedIn: www.linkedin.com/in/cathryn-finley

9. ~~FAKE~~ FAITH IT 'TIL YOU MAKE IT
BY KRISTI ELLISON SMITH

Have you ever felt like an imposter? Not in a fraudulent way, but more like a fish out of water? You distinctively remember buying a ticket for the bullet train to success, but now you feel you might have accidentally gotten on an old steam engine? Why on earth does it feel like there are so many detours? Shouldn't someone have given you a detailed map to follow? When we find ourselves unsure of which direction to turn along our entrepreneurial journey, we must lean hard on our faith to help us arrive safely.

The first time this feeling hit me was my first job out of grad school. Fresh faced and eager to impress, in my best suit and new shoes that cost a month's pay; I vividly remember walking down the hallway that first day on cloud nine, excitement and anticipation bubbling inside. Well, uncertainty quickly engulfed my enthusiasm as I learned that I would be spending my first weeks in "the pit," a training ground for newbies used by upper management to determine who had the skills needed to make the cut. There were hours of cold calls, role-plays, reviewing your recorded sessions with management and being taught how to respond to situations *more* effectively. Considering my life experience to date, the pit was *high* stress and held high expectations. Running drills and getting constantly critiqued was not quite what I had envisioned for myself. I remember questioning God's plan, wanting to make certain *this* is what He meant for me to be doing. I could feel God respond, *stay the course*. I did, and upon graduating from the pit, I received my own territory.

As the new kid on the block, I was given our least cultivated territory. We had virtually no market presence. Business was difficult to procure and tricky regulatory issues added to the challenge. The majority of my salary was commission based, and I knew to make this work for my family and me, I was going to have to pray like it depended on God and work like it depended on me. And I did.

I recognized that I needed a plan that would help me become more visible in my market and the telephone was the most effective channel in the industry at that time. Every day I made 75-100 cold calls to people who hadn't heard of our company and certainly didn't know who I was. I had to develop a style of credibility in my conversations with people that lead them to transfer me to those who could make buying decisions. This was tedious and time-consuming, but once the business was secured, there was an opportunity for residual commissions.

I faced a great deal of rejection that first year, building relationships and establishing both our brand and myself in the market. Many times it felt like pushing a boulder uphill. During peak times of frustration, I would habitually confirm with God that this was still my path, even though I knew the answer hadn't changed, *stay the course*. So I did. I remained self-disciplined, heeding my mentors' advice and holding myself to the high standards I knew were essential for success. I held faith in His plan knowing that as long as I stood in His will; He would not lead me astray.

Mindset work became imperative. I imagined myself already having accomplished my goals. God had placed me in this position for a reason, and I worked for His glory daily. I had faith in the talents and skills that He gave to me (Romans 12:6) and that I would use them to the best of my ability. I persevered and in the end, it became one of my most rewarding years as I was awarded the Rookie of the Year Award and doubled my salary.

Pro Tips: Faith*full* Mindset

- Have confidence that you are perfectly positioned and exclusively assigned by God to be exactly where you are. He has very important work for you to do! Move boldly, with assurance and trust in His plan.

- Focus on working for God, not man. (Colossians 3:23-24). Clarity and creativity will improve on ideas that are aligned with God's will, and others will fade or not take flight.

- Imagine that you are already successful! This one is extremely important. God wants big, abundant blessings for us. (Jeremiah 29:11) Picture yourself having accomplished your goals, daily. Declare your future success now!

The Unintended Entrepreneur

Some believe you are either born an entrepreneur or you are not. I didn't grow up dreaming of owning my own business, and I never felt constricted by corporate America, in fact, I found it quite rewarding. It was never *my* plan; however, God and life-events carved a path that led me to become what I like to call an *unintended entrepreneur*.

After 18-hours of labor with my first child, we realized her cord was wrapped around her neck three times. Unbelievable anxiety consumed us, but we were thankfully blessed with a successful delivery. Shortly after, fear hit again when we discovered I was internally hemorrhaging. Following surgery and life-saving transfusions, I was finally cleared to go home with our beautiful newborn. Like most new moms, I survived the first few blurry months on hormones and adrenaline as we healed together. That experience changed me. For the first time, I was fully responsible for someone else and for the first time I had been faced with my own mortality. I knew He saved me for a purpose; His purpose.

Maternity leave ended, and the first business flight away was heart wrenching. It got easier, though, as I adjusted into a routine. I did not have the yearning to be a stay at home mom that many of my friends had, even after our second child. For a decade, I collected promotions, raises, and certifications. I felt fulfilled and accomplished, both professionally and in my family life.

So imagine my surprise when I began sensing a change in my spirit and a new longing to be at home! Over the years, the rush I had once felt preparing for executive meetings, pushing against deadlines and climbing the corporate ladder had slowly dissipated and the feeling that I was missing special moments in my children's lives grew. Looking back, I recognized every position I had held was prepping me for the next. I had learned so many lessons during my journey, and I understood that God had been grooming me and guiding me down this path. In gratitude and understanding, I prayed for direction. Soon after, a respected friend contacted me to talk about an opportunity that had blessed her family, and I was uncharacteristically receptive to listening.

I remember going home that night after listening to my friend, my head spinning with excitement. I contemplated my current situation, wondering *what if* there was a way that I could use my God-given talents to help others, to both make a living *and* be home with my family. Dare I dream and allow myself to become excited about the possibility? After all, this prospect was not packaged the way I had expected, nor was it something I would have ever initiated on my own. I believed God had placed this opportunity in front of me for a reason. After much consideration, research, and prayer, I truly felt the only risk was in not pursuing it.

But What If I Fail?

As entrepreneurs, we must learn how to navigate through

uncertainty. Starting a new business can be scary! Launching a new product, shooting a video, writing a book, or booking a speaking-engagement takes courage. Satan is lurking, awaiting any opportunity to sabotage and place self-doubt in our minds. He uses fear to hinder us from reaching our full potential. Remember that fear is NOT of God. When you know you are walking in God's will, move forward in spite of fear, knowing that God is by your side (Isaiah 41:10).

Pro Tips: *Banishing Fear*

- When you feel fear creeping in, refocus your thoughts on gratitude for the opportunity. For example, if you are feeling intimidated by a speaking engagement, express gratitude for the opportunity to share your message and trust that God will open the hearts of those who need to receive what you offer. Keep a gratitude journal so that you have a recorded history of being thankful for what you have. This practice will attract positive outcomes. Try it and see.

- Cultivate relationships with people who support your goals and dreams. It's okay to put space between you and Negative Nancy or Doubting Thomas. My dad always reminded me "You are the average of the five friends that you spend the most time with." How does your tribe look? If they are not lifting you up, it is time to re-evaluate.

- Eliminate destructive thoughts and replace negative self-talk with positive affirmations. Speak your affirmations out loud for at least five minutes, three times a day. Example: if you feel stuck in your ability to book new clients, repeatedly tell yourself "I attract highly qualified clients who see extreme value in the services I offer and are excited to work with me."

Intentions versus Actions

There is a parable you may have heard about two sons. A father asks his first son to go and work in the vineyard and although the son says no, the son eventually decides to go and do the work. The father asks his second son to work as well, and although that son says he *will* work in the vineyard, he never shows. Which of the two sons honored what their father wanted? The son who did the work. (Matthew 21:28-32)

Entrepreneurs sometimes have a natural propensity to identify with the behavior of the second son. With our minds brimming with momentous ideas and intentions, it can be easy to fail in following through with the necessary behaviors and required actions. Desiring results without taking action leads us down a road littered with excuses, self-doubt, and fear. When God opens a door for you, honor the opportunity and take action.

Pro Tips: *Up-level Your Game*

- Get going! If you want to change an outcome, you must first change the investment. Conduct an honest evaluation and determine if your current actions align with the goals that you have set for yourself. Move past fear and allow yourself grace: you aren't expected to be as successful out of the gate as someone who's been in the game awhile. Remember, *they started somewhere too*! Honor where *you* are in *your* journey and keep moving!

- Make a vision board and use it to bring your dreams to life! There are no rules on what you can add, so attach anything and everything that inspires or motivates you: include pictures, inspirational quotes, future titles and goals that you want to achieve.
    - How large do you want your company to be? Do you want to add a product or service line? Do you want to earn enough revenue to support a charity or

create a foundation? Do you want to transition your brick and mortar business online? Are you franchising? How do you want your life to look in one, three, and five years? What will you do with your time and resources? Add items to your vision board that represent your desired future.

o Your business plan should align with your vision board. Establish timeframes, short and long term goals. Be specific!

- Know your priorities and tackle your top priorities first. Focus on actions that both align with your vision board and generate revenue for your company.

Entrepreneurs experience a rollercoaster of emotions as they navigate their path. It comes with the territory. Permit your faith to guide you and believe you were exclusively chosen to run *your* business and share it with others. Keep a faithful mindset and have the courage to move past fear. Faith is the catalyst that provides you with the confidence, self-discipline and drive required for success. And one last little secret: even though we may experience wild success, we never should allow ourselves to believe that we've "made it" because there is *always* more work to be done.

ABOUT KRISTI ELLISON SMITH

Kristi Smith is an entrepreneur, inspirational life and business mentor who believes that when women step into the full purpose that God designed for them and unite together in community, divine transformations emerge. Her passion is for helping women by propelling their God sized dreams into reality, providing trusted leadership and sound business advice that honors the journey above all. She teaches that our lives so far have been a series of steps leading to the present moment, and that each day we have the opportunity to step out, embrace faith in our higher purpose and make bold decisions that shatter the status quo. A self-described 'recovering perfectionist', she has traversed as many roads in business as she has personally, and knows first-hand how the *power of yes* can change everything.

Featured in over 350 publications, including ABC, NBC, CBS, FOX, Wall Street Select, The Boston Globe and CEOWorld Magazine, Kristi holds a double major in Business Management and Marketing from Texas A&M University and a Masters of Business Administration from the University of Dallas along with multiple professional certifications but her ultimate reward comes from the connections she makes with others and seeing their joy as they experience breakthroughs through faith and renewal. Proud to live and work in her hometown of Dallas, Texas, she's a devoted wife and mother to two children whose own lives have been an unforeseen journey and a step-out in faith.

CONTACT KRISTI ELLISON SMITH

Website: www.xokristi.com

Email: kristi@xokristi.com

Phone: 1-844-KRISTI-1

Facebook: https://www.facebook.com/xokristismith

Twitter: @xokristismith

Free Offer: Imagine if you could start every day with positive, affirming words that fill your spirit and enrich your life. Your day would be brighter, your head held higher and your confidence renewed. This continued practice would propel you toward your goals. You would envision yourself achieving them. You would become Godfident! Visit my website for your free offer.

10. IF YOU DON'T SET A GODLY STANDARD, WHO WILL?
BY CHERYL LENAMON

One of the greatest things about being "the boss" is you get to set the standard, whether you head up a company or are an entrepreneur working with a team of people. But in today's marketplace, what is that standard? And more to the point, what is your standard? As shifting morals and political correctness dominate, can a Godly standard be set much less maintained long-term?

Looking back over my career as an entrepreneur and business owner, I can see clearly some God ordained standards He helped me to understand, implement and sustain throughout my life. My prayer is they will help you grow your relationship with Him and your business as a Spirit Fed Entrepreneur.

Standard #1: Choose Wisely

None of us can set and maintain a fearlessly high standard without making choices. And sometimes those choices are tough. If you are relying on feelings, emotions or fear, the choices you make will let you down. I guarantee it.

For so many years, I made the dumbest, most self-destructive choices possible. In fact, I wrote a book, *Potholes & Pigsties, a Prodigal's Journey Home* after God shook me out of my stupor and showed me what I was doing to myself, my family and my life.

One important thing I learned was without absolutes in my life; my standards changed based on the circumstances and situations in my life. I began searching for a way to find consistency and value. I found that through studying God's Word. That may sound easier than it was because I've always been someone who can see multiple sides of any discussion, disagreement or solution. Before understanding the absolutes of God's truth, I had never been a black or white person; I saw and responded in tones of gray. Absolutes were foreign to me. But as I studied, I began to understand how these absolute truths intertwined and worked together to form principles and standards I could build, not only my life, on but also my business.

Standard #2: Fearless Business & Financial Integrity

"We need to be very careful doing businesses with individuals and companies who openly declare themselves, "Christians," I told my staff in our weekly meeting. Sadly, it had come to that. As an owner of a small business, I had determined we couldn't afford any more late payments or bad debts. After being in business for ten successful years, the only clients who had caused us grief were Christians, and I was upset, frustrated and a little bit angry.

The first time it happened was after a newly formed Christian publishing company called us in to design several book covers and a promotional campaign for their upcoming releases. Having worked with Word Publishing for several years, my ad agency was experienced in the Christian publishing market, so the projects were a good fit for our designers. During my first meeting, I met with the president and founder of the company for an hour as he told me how God had directed him on this course and led him to start the publishing company. The following week I returned with a cost estimate and an invoice for one-third down payment to start the project. The bid was accepted, the down payment made and the owner pushed me to rush the project.

Unfortunately, as the owner prayed for God to supply the money he did not have, we finished the work and waited...and waited... and waited. The money never came and after a year, the publishing company closed owing most of their vendors. The owner was humiliated, and his testimony was lost and never recovered.

After a few of these experiences, I began asking for money upfront only to be told my faith in God was lacking. But my faith in God was not lacking, it was my faith in many Christian business owners that was lacking.

I've heard it all: "God has told me to do this, and so I know the money will come." "I am stepping out in faith, knowing God will provide." "Be my partner to evangelize the world – together we will make the difference, and God will provide the income."

Sorry, I have learned God usually doesn't work that way. And unfortunately, the businesses hurt because of late, or no payment for services done, or products provided are left holding the bag and feeling duped. Not a good testimony for sure.

I determined early on as an owner of a business paying bills promptly and not overextending myself would be a priority. I was extremely blessed by running a company that honored God, but I knew I had to be a good steward of the money. I understood my financial reputation in the community was a testament to Him, and hurting that reputation hurt not only my testimony as a Christian but my relationship with Jesus.

Standard #3: Honesty and Integrity Start at the Top and Trickle Down.

As a business owner with over twenty employees, I thought I understood my responsibility of setting the standards for honesty. If I lied to clients or vendors, so would my staff. I remember vividly one day telling my receptionist to tell a client I wasn't in. I was feverishly writing the copy for an annual report, and I didn't want to talk to anyone until I had completed my task. My receptionist said, "I'm not going to lie for you." Boy, did that hit me like a ton of bricks. I had actually told her to lie, after me being the archangel of truth in my agency. Sure, it was a little "white lie" and yes, I would talk to this client in just a few hours, but in that second of letting down my guard I had done exactly what I told my staff never to do, and I wasn't walking the talk.

Living a life submitted to the Spirit is easy when you are at church or see others only occasionally. It's much harder in an office environment or with a family who see you each day – at your best and your worst. The responsibility that comes with that is overwhelming at times, especially if you are being "watched" by unbelievers who are just waiting to pounce when you fail. I learned the only way to deal with that pressure was to be transparent. To humble myself when I was wrong and to admit openly my weaknesses. I learned that people were a lot more forgiving when you are vulnerable. After the "lying" episode with my receptionist, I apologized to her and told her I would never, ever do that again. I was busted! And I have never forgotten how in a moment of selfishness I had harmed my Christian testimony with her.

Fortunately, I love people. So, it's generally easy for me to be nice and to treat others as I would want to be treated. I know that is not easy for everyone, and I am eternally grateful that God put people-love in my DNA. Probably because of that, I truly appreciated what each of my staff and clients brought to the table. I genuinely cared for them, and it didn't matter how big a client they were, or what they could do for me, I wanted to give them my best. I wanted them to know, I had their best interest at heart, and I encouraged that from my staff. If anything, we gave far more than was expected or paid for, and in that way, we were able to show forth our honesty and integrity.

Standard #4: Surround Yourself with People of Like Values

Paramount to establishing a team with not only talent but the integrity I grew to want, happened in the selection process. It's very tempting to hire a top talent, but if that talent does not mesh with your company's core values, you've got trouble. Eventually, I learned that integrity trumped talent. Was I always successful? No. I had a few missteps along the way. I lost a good client because a designer showed up stoned for a photography shoot. (Who knew?) I had to tap dance on a few tables to convince another client that an account executive who lied about missing a deadline was now on probation and going through additional training (which by the way, didn't work and he was later laid off). But in the twenty years of owning my agency, those incidences were rare, and I learned valuable lessons along the way.

I learned in the beginning when my faith was weaker, being around people of lower moral standards tended to bring me down a notch or two; I wasn't able to bring them up.

I learned I craved acceptance and didn't like to make waves, so would compromise to fit it.

I learned how deeply I respected people who were consistent in their actions and values.

As I grew in my spiritual maturity, I realized how much we need each other. People of like values can hold each other up, stand in the gap for one another and be accountable to each other. These relationships can make all the difference in maintaining Godly standards for the long term.

So my best advice to Spirit-Fed Entrepreneurs is to choose wisely, be fearless in your business and financial integrity, be honest and surround yourself with people of like values. If you do, God will honor your choices and bless you abundantly more than you could ever imagine.

ABOUT CHERYL LENAMON

Cheryl Lenamon, owner of Bright Idea Content, is an award-winning copywriter, author of *Potholes & Pigsties*, *A Prodigal's Journey Home* and a digital marketing professional with years of business experience. Owning a successful Ad Agency with national clients in diverse industries challenged her to deliver bright, compelling and innovative copy that sells. Prior to opening Bright Idea Content in 2014, she spent the past few years in the digital marketing world creating campaigns for national and international clients. While her skills are diverse, her passion remains the same. She brings the art of rich content to life in the voice of her client.

Cheryl is married to Ronnie and lives in Waco Texas. When she isn't writing, she teaches Precept Bible Classes at Highland Baptist Church, walks her dogs, loves on her cats, creates artsy crafts and enjoys life.

CONTACT CHERYL LENAMON

Email: cheryl@brightideacontent.com
Facebook: https://www.facebook.com/cheryl.lenamon.7
Twitter: @BrightIContent
LinkedIn: www.linkedin.com/in/cheryllenamon/

Website: Visit www.brightideacontent.com to learn more about Cheryl, hear what customers say and see her work.

11. IS YOUR SELF-IMAGE SABATOGING YOUR SUCCESS?
BY BRUCE MAZZARRE

If you've ever wondered why it's hard to increase your productivity/performance long-term after being pumped up in a mastermind group or training workshop, you are not alone. Research has shown the four billion dollars spent yearly on training is only 15 to 20 percent effective.

The question is why? Why do many of us take the initiative to learn how to do a better job, and then take that information and increase our performance short-term, only to slide back to where we were before the training? National research conducted by a group of psychologists points to a growth model they call the Identity Role Barrier. This barrier proves we can't outperform beyond what we believe we can see in ourselves. In other words, our self-image affects our performance long-term; a low self-concept diminishes the results of skill training.

So, let's take a look at the Identity/Role Barrier.

IDENTITY/ROLE BARRIER

Training

Low 1 2 3 4 5 6 7 8 9 10 High

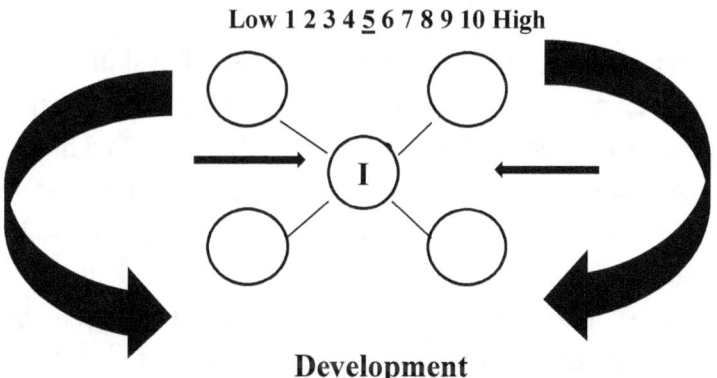

Development

Low 1 2 3 4 5 6 7 8 9 10 High

As you can see in this diagram, there is an "I" in the center which stands for Identify, often called self-concept or self-image. This "I" is how we see ourselves. The "R's" surrounding the "I" stand for the various roles in our lives. These roles could be a business owner, parent, spouse, friend, civic leader, Sunday school teacher, small group leader and so on. Let's face it, we all play multiple roles every day. All those roles then are tied to our identity or self-concept.

Here's how understanding the Identity/Role Barrier can help you succeed.

I've spent my business career developing entrepreneurs or management leaders either one-on-one or in organizational structures. Many times I take them through the Identity/Role

Barrier exercise, and I ask managers or entrepreneurs to rate the mental image they have of themselves on a 1 to 10 scale, 10 being the highest. (This mental image includes their perception of their strengths, weaknesses, status, etc.) I've been amazed how low many see themselves in terms of identity or self-concept. On average, their scores are a 4 or 5, and because of this low number they tend to perform at that level.

Prior to this exercise, my clients have all invested in skill training. And have been concerned that many times their training has not brought the results they were looking for. After spending money on expensive workshops or training sessions for management/staff they see performance levels increase initially only to slide back and plateau over time. In fact, after training, an individual performance score might be as high as 9 on our 1 to 10 scale, but as time goes by, their performance score drops to exactly where their self-concept score was, a 4 or a 5. These organizations have been left with a choice, either send the individuals for more training or hire new people to replace those performing at a substandard level. Either way, it is an expensive proposition for any organization.

The same thing happens to entrepreneurs and solopreneurs. Let's take Marlena; she's a Christian solopreneur who introduced a new God-centered wellness product to the market last year. Her considerable expertise in health and fitness is propelling her forward, but her performance on the sales side of her business is a cause for alarm. Marlena wants to succeed and has spent thousands of dollars with various coaches and expensive training sessions. After each session, workshop or conference, her productivity increased significantly. In fact, on a scale from 1 to 10, Marlena was performing at a 9. She was motivated, networked successfully and knew how to sell her product, but as months went by Marlena's performance slipped and sales fell flat.

Why can't Marlena maintain the "9" performance rating she realized after her training?

Here's what happened. Marlena's self-concept is a 5, but her training boosted her confidence to a 9 – but only for a short while. Gradually her performance slipped, and she started performing as a 5. So, what does Marlena do? She goes for more training. She attends another workshop for additional training, and the cycle repeats itself.

So, should Marlena save her money on additional training? No, I am all for continuing training and education. Training is necessary, but it's only half of the equation. Here's the solution to Marlena's issue: she needs to develop her self-concept along with skill training. If she doesn't, she will eventually lose confidence and give up on her business. According to Forbes, 90% of all startups fail for various reasons, and Marlena earnestly wants to be part of the 10% who not only make it, but thrive.

I am rooting for Marlena. I am also a big believer in prayer and the power of the Holy Spirit to work within all believers. After all, He is our ultimate teacher, and I have seen HIM in action. A good example of this is a writer friend of mine who started her one-woman, home-based company in 2014. As her self-concept grew, she began taking on assignments which she believed were beyond her capabilities. Before each project, she prays for guidance, creativity and without fail, her performance exceeds what she thought she could do. She began by writing blogs and websites, and now edits books and is a ghostwriter for many successful authors. With each challenging assignment, her confidence grows, but she never forgets where to go for a healthy boost of self-concept.

As Christian believers, we have THE source for supreme confidence. Our identity is ultimately tied to who we are in Christ.

Just the thought that we are kids of the KING should be enough, but sadly we all too often listen to the other voices in our head. The ones telling us we are not good enough, we'll never succeed. Many people can never get beyond that and the self-defeating mantra playing over and over again in their minds.

Can we silence that mantra? You bet we can. As we begin to gain confidence in the roles we perform, whether that be in business or daily life within our community or church, our Identity increases. As our Identity increases, so does our performance.

The key is to add identity-development as much as skill training to break the Identity/Role Barrier. We can do this through prayer, reading, enrichment counseling or coaching. Just understanding this concept is a major step in the right direction. And the great part is, when your identity is boosted your entire life including your relationships will be enriched. You will become a better parent, a better spouse and a better friend. I have seen it become a reality within businesses I consult with and with entrepreneurs and solopreneurs I coach.

If you would like to learn more about my identity-development process, please contact me for a free consultation.

ABOUT BRUCE MAZZARRE

Founder & CEO of Management Development System
Author of *Winning Performance Library*, a series of online courses
for personal, career and business development.

As with most people, my life is spent in a series of roles I involve
myself in on a daily basis. I am a husband to Carol, a father to
Mark and Monica, and a grandfather to six. Away from my home,
I take on the role of business owner. My company, Management
Development System is based in Texas and has been going strong
for 30 years. In addition, I take an enthusiast role applying
Kingdom principles to the workplace, and host a weekly business
men's group based on these principles. One of my favorite roles is
as a mentor to young men and women who have an entrepreneurial
spirit, and to couples who are seeking Christ-centered
relationships. While mentoring is extremely fulfilling, one of my
most interesting roles was overseeing missionaries in third world
countries as they sought to develop business opportunities as part
of their ministry. I am fully aware every role I play has a purpose
in God's economy as I seek to better lives through personal and
career development. To see what I do in my business role go to
www.assessmentsolutions.com.

CONTACT BRUCE MAZZARRE

LinkedIn: https://www.linkedin.com/in/brucemazzarrare

Facebook: https://www.facebook.com/managementdevelopmentsystems/

Twitter: @brucemaz

Website: assessmentsolutions.com

Email: bmazzare@assessmentsolutions.com

Phone: 254-776-6306

12. LIVING IN THE GODFLOW
BY ANGELA SLADEN DE ROX

"...and where the Spirit of the Lord is, there is freedom."

(2 Corinthians 3:17)

From the age of seven, I grew up in a Bible-believing church that understood and practiced community. It was a normal part of our evening to take a walk and stop in for coffee somewhere along the way or end up being the recipients of coffee guests. We were a mixed community of Christ followers: European, Canadian Indian, and Asian.

We learned all the do's and don'ts of the Bible and tried really hard to follow them. They were reinforced at home, school, out in the community, and in church – there was no escaping the consequences of our wrongdoing. A great foundation of faith was laid for me, and I am grateful.

I did not, however, learn what freedom meant nor the power of liberty in our walk with God and that freedom was the whole intention of the Gospel: to bring freedom into every part of our lives. I have come to call this life of freedom "the God Flow," and it encompasses four main themes: **F**reedom, **L**ove, **O**pportunity, and **W**illingness.

We are in the God Flow anytime we choose to walk in the Spirit. As a young believer, I did not understand what it truly meant to walk in the Spirit and assumed it was for the super-spiritual people – people who were really good at keeping all the do's and don'ts – which I very much wasn't capable of doing. Instead of freedom, I was plagued with guilt, shame, and condemnation. I couldn't understand how "there is therefore now NO condemnation for those in Christ Jesus." Either they were perfect, or I wasn't in Christ Jesus.

So, in an effort to try and try again, I became more determined to be a "good girl." I was sincere in my efforts and put on a good show; I led worship in our church, homeschooled my ten children, raised my children in the Word, led Bible studies, guarded my children from the evil in music and on TV, had my own daily Bible study and prayer time, listened to great messages, was faithful to my husband, kept myself and my family healthy, and was active in the Pro-Life Movement. I was well-respected and "had it all."

It came all tumbling down around me in 2009 when I made some life-changing decisions that caused me to lose the respect of my family, children and church community. I didn't just fall off my spiritual pedestal: I came crashing down. I won't go into the details of what happened or why; it's not important anymore. What is important is what happened after and how God, in His incredible mercy, showed me how to truly live in relationship with Him and how trying to have a relationship with Him apart from His plan will never work. It was my "doing" that got me in trouble. Spiritual pride set in and it separated me from God, and He allowed me to be totally stripped of all my pride in a matter of weeks. I am forever grateful. I am not proud of how my "fall" happened, but I am eternally grateful for the process the Lord brought me through when I was broken and had come to the end of "myself."

The first thing the Lord taught me was what *Freedom* was — what it meant to be truly free. I was in a very lonely, shameful and guilt-ridden place – the ultimate place all my self-righteousness had brought me. Stripped of all honor, I had nothing left to stand on or have people admire me for any more. This was the beginning of freedom. The only thing I had was God and a burning desire to know Him. I'd heard about other people having an incredible, intimate relationship with God but had never experienced it myself. I was out of "good works,"so it was just God and I now, and He began to show me what it meant to be free – free from the approval of man, free from the constant struggle to "be" perfect, free from fear, free to trust, and free to rest and let go of all striving.

God truly showed me "Where the Spirit of the Lord is, there is freedom" (2 Corinthians 3:17). This has become my life's motto and what I now strive for. The Greek root word for freedom is *eleuthena* which means 'the license to live as we should and not as we please.' It is the exact opposite definition of freedom most people have – to live as one pleases. What is beautiful about this verse is it says nothing about our effort to live as we please: it is the direct effect of living in the God Flow – with the Spirit. It is not something we *do*; it is something we choose to *invite* into our lives: The Spirit of God. Jesus tells us in Luke 11:13 that the heavenly Father is willing, even excited, to give the Holy Spirit to them that ask. The Spirit is not something we can earn; it is a gift from the Father, and we have to ask for it. The more we ask, the more we get.

The God Flow is powered by God, and God is **Love**. ***"Now these three remain: faith, hope and love – but the greatest of these is love," (1 Corinthians 13:13)***. As a little girl, I memorized the fruit of the Spirit as listed in Galatians 5: love, joy, peace, patience, kindness, gentleness, goodness, faithfulness, and self-control. I tried in my own power to be all those things but fell in at least one of them every day. What I discovered in the process of God "turning my story into His glory" was that it was not my job, or even in my abilities, to love or live out the fruit of the Spirit. It was not my fruit, I did not own it, and I did not have the power to express it in my own flesh. However, the more I ask for God's Spirit to manifest in my life, the more I am able to walk in love which encompasses all the other fruit as well. Because God is Love, when I invite more of His Spirit into my life, the more I operate in love.

The God Flow is God's plan for our lives. In that plan, He presents opportunities for us to serve. Jesus was the perfect example of what it looks like to live your life in the God Flow. Matthew 4:23 tells us that ***"He went about . . . teaching, preaching, and healing . . . among the people."*** The Greek definition of the word "heal" in this verse means 'to serve, do service, and/or restore to health.' The interesting thing about Jesus' walk was that He didn't go looking for people to heal; they came to Him, or He met them along His journey. His Father presented opportunities for Him to serve, to heal, and He did. He would stop in the middle of whatever He was doing to serve. People came first, people mattered most, and people were the priority.

To truly live in the God Flow means we are open to the **Opportunity** to serve others whom God puts in our path. We don't have to look for them; He will bring them to us. When we begin to see service to others as a blessing and privilege and not as a nuisance or interruption, then we are partnering with God in His work on the Earth: we become His feet, His hands, His mouth, His ears and His touch. What a blessing and honor!

One side note about serving. In the midst of all my serving, I got so tied up in the *actions* of serving that I forgot *whom* I was serving. Serving can become a god instead of a response to the serving opportunities God brings to us. Oswald Chambers says it so well: "The call of God is not a call to any particular service; my interpretation of it may be because contact with the nature of God has made me realize what I would like to do for Him." God created you with your gifts, talents, passions and personality. He knows which people to bring to you who will give you an opportunity to serve them and/or to continue to develop you. Keep your eyes open to where the Lord leads you and to whom He leads you. These are great opportunities.

Finally, the God Flow is **Willingness**. If there is any work to living in the God Flow, this is it. The God Flow goes against all that is human nature – it is the "upside-down" kingdom. If you want to lead, serve. If you are persecuted, pray for your persecutor. If you need more money, give it away. If you want to save your life, lay it down. If you want to be first, choose to be last. We have to be willing to live life with an open hand, so to speak. Own nothing as it all belongs to God anyway. Forget about *personal* development and focus on *Spirit* development. Walk by faith, not by sight. Seek *first* the kingdom of God and He will take care of everything else.

All this goes against our need to control our life, circumstances, and our destiny. To truly live in the God Flow, we must be willing to hold very loosely to everything we feel is ours and hold very tightly to God, His plans for us (even though we don't know what they are until they unfold), and His promise that He will never leave us nor forsake us. This requires us to make a conscious choice and *to will* ourselves to live in the God Flow.

In conclusion, I invite you to join me on this exciting journey called the God Flow. The path is narrow, dark (you can't see beyond where you are at any present moment), and rarely traveled. You are provided with a Light (God's Word), a Guide (the Holy Spirit) who will tell you to "turn here" or "turn there," and the Promise that the One, who created the path, will bring you safely to the end. You can't control the direction or even the pace at which you travel; it is all decided for you. BUT, you will walk with the Creator of the universe and participate in His plan for the Earth. You will fulfill your true destiny and do what only you can do.

No one can do what God has planned for you to do, just as you cannot do what God has planned for another to do. The rewards are eternal, and the cost is everything you've got and everything you are, but you will become all that God intends you to be. In the God Flow, you will live the most fulfilling, exciting and rewarding life — more than you can even think or imagine. The adventure of adventures awaits you!

ABOUT ANGELA SLADEN DE ROX

Angela Sladen-de Rox, Certified General & Sports
Nutritionist and owner of Total Health Method for almost 20 years,
lives with her husband, David, (and several friends who come and
go when they need a place to hang their hat for a few weeks or
months) on their private, quiet acreage outside of Sherwood Park,
Alberta, Canada; the perfect location from which to run her
business.

Angela, like most women, wears many hats, and happily. She is
"mom" to 10 very independent children (6 boys, 4 girls; 5
biological and 5 foster) and grandma to 10 of the most talented
grandchildren on the earth...no bias of course.

She has helped 1000's of individuals change their *health* and
improve athletic performance by focusing on Nutritional
Cleansing. Angela has also trained 100's of individuals, globally,
to change their wealth by building a successful home-based
business. She is passionate about helping relieve others of
physical and financial pain.

Angela has also owned and managed several businesses related to helping women and is now, in partnership with her husband, the Managing Director of the Edmonton and Calgary WGLA chapters.

She also loves to write and share her "Godflow" story with the hopes of inspiring others to follow their "Godflow".

CONTACT ANGELA SLADEN de ROX

Websites: www.totalhealthmethod.com,

www.transformation90.com,

www.bodyrebootsystem.com

www.thegodflow.com

Email: angela@reachangela.com

Phone: 780-717-8296

Social Media: https://www.facebook.com/angelasladenderox

https://ca.linkedin.com/in/angelasladen

https://twitter.com/AngelaSladen

Free Offer: Download Angela's free ebook, "The ABC's of Physical and Financial Health" on her website www.reaCHANGEla.com

13. TURNING PAIN INTO POWER
AND GRIEF INTO PEACE
BY ANGELA ALEXANDER

Angela's "back to Jesus moment" occurred when the doctor said, "You'll probably be a widow by Christmas." That was Dec. 3, 1985.

At twenty-four Angela's husband, Sgt. Surie Alexander, suffered a severe brain aneurysm. Immediately he could not read, write, talk, and no longer knew the alphabet. They were evacuated from Germany to Walter Reed Hospital where Surie had an eighteen-hour brain surgery. The doctors tried to prepare Angela by saying, "There's a possibility your husband may not survive. If he does he could be paralyzed, have a totally different personality, or possibly have amnesia. One thing we know for sure is, he'll never be the man you married last year."

Surie survived! After another five-hour surgery and eight long months in the hospital the military honorably and medically retired him from the Army.

For years, Angela took her husband to speech therapy. Eventually, they had two children named Angela and Murice. The Alexanders were so grateful for Surie's quality of life that they wanted to give back in a tangible way. They became a foster family to Angelina and Roger. When Murice and Roger met one another, it was instantaneous love. They were truly brothers from a different mother, but our same Heavenly Father!

As a result of Surie's improvements in his speech and cognitive skills, Angela reactivated her Air Force Reserve career.

We all know that God is good all the time, and all the time God is good! Well, Angela truly believe that statement even on her darkest day.

On April 1, 2000, while Angela was in Japan on military duty, she was working with a group of people. Lt. Mevehichi said,

"Alexander I need to speak with you." It was April Fool's weekend, so her guard went up. She didn't want to be the joke of the day. They began walking and talking about nothing. They entered a small office. Inside was a man who was introduced as a priest, and a female from their unit. The priest began nervously reading paperwork from the Red Cross. He said, "Angela, your family has been in a car accident." From the looks on their faces, she knew this was no April's Fool's Joke!

The day before, Surie and their four children were driving down a highway in California. A car cut them off. Their truck hit the center divider, upon impact everyone was knocked unconscious. Their truck went backward across the highway, fell twenty-five feet below, and landed upside down on top of two parked vehicles with people inside. Praise God their truck fell on their engine and not their roof! The people in those vehicles were extremely shaken up, but they were alright.

Most people thought by Angela being on the other side of the world that it would be the worst place possible. She expressed that she needed to be that far away in order to hear God's voice, because if she were home, she would have run somewhere. In Japan, she had no choice, but to be still and know that God is still God. Because whenever and wherever there's a crisis, Christ is.

The priest said,

"Your husband Surie, he's in the hospital, but he's okay."

"Your daughter Angela, she's in the hospital, but she's okay."

"Your daughter Angelina, she's in the hospital, but she's okay."

"Your two eight-year-old sons, Murice and Roger, they didn't make it."

Instantly, as if only God and Angela were in the room, she recalled a prayer her children said before going to bed.

"Now I lay me down to sleep,

I pray the Lord, my soul to keep.

If I should die before, I wake,

I pray the Lord, my soul to take."

Maybe because she wanted to hear from her sons so badly, she felt in her heart as if she heard them say, "No, Mommy, that priest is wrong. We prayed the Lord, our soul to take. We did make it! We're here with J-e-s-u-s!"

God was sending her so much love, and so much peace; there was no room for pain. The people in the room were watching and waiting for her world to turn upside down. Instead, they witnessed her world still in alignment with the One we call our Heavenly Father, our Prince of Peace, our Comforter and Provider, the Almighty God!

The next day on her plane ride to Los Angeles, Angela kept pinching herself. She couldn't believe she still knew the alphabet, her address, the date. Previously when asked, she said she would go crazy if something happened to her children. When that didn't happen, she knew God had interceded on her behalf. Angela said she read about peace that surpasses your understanding, but never experienced that peace until her sons passed. In the midst of her storm she first praised God that her whole family hadn't passed away. She thanked God that Murice and Roger passed instantly. Absent from the body is present with the Lord. She thanked God they weren't hooked up to a life-support machine, suffering, waiting for her to come home, only then to pass away.

Her eleven-year-old daughter Angela required ten staples in her knee. Angelina ten-years-old suffered a minor shoulder injury. Surie hit his head; he had a concussion! Instantly, all those years of speech therapy, occupational therapy, and physical therapy were go-n-e, gone. When the police heard his slurred voice, they assumed he was on drugs and/or alcohol and were ready to take him straight to jail. His daughter Angela said, "Oh no, my father had a brain aneurysm!" The problem was she lost her credibility a long time ago when she said her mother was in Japan. They didn't believe a single word she said.

About an hour later into the flight, Angela almost set straight up in her seat when she recalled a letter Murice had written about a month before the car crash. Murice was in the 3rd grade; he had a math test at school. He finished early and received his 'A'. While he was waiting for his classmates to complete their test, he wrote a letter to his parents. Murice had never written them a letter before. Murice ran in the house that afternoon from school and shouted, "Mommy, Daddy, I wrote you a letter!" They sat at the foot of their bed and read his letter aloud. Murice letter not only expressed that he loved them, he explained why he loved them, and at the end of all three pages, he wrote, "*by-by.*"

The Thursday before their double memorial service, Angela stood in her kitchen and cried, and prayed, and cried.

Dear God,

Thank you so much for Murice's incredible good-bye letter, it's truly the reason I can stand here right now. However, I need to know that Roger was at peace. I need to know that he was also visited by the Holy Spirit . . .

Suddenly Angela felt one word in her spirit, and that word was search. Angela searched her home for over three hours that afternoon but didn't find anything that gave her the peace that she had prayed for.

Only as God can create it! Only as God can orchestrate it! That evening was open house at her children's school. They eventually entered Roger's second-grade class. Two weeks before the car crash Mrs. Blassey had given all of her students all kinds of arts and craft supplies, and said, "Do something for open-house because your parents are coming," with no other instructions. God designed this opportunity for Roger to write and leave his good-bye letter.

All of their projects were stapled to the wall. Angela retrieved Roger's letter from the wall and instantly she knew this is what she had been searching and believing for. Angela almost fell to her knees as she thanked God for answering her prayers. Both letters were written above and beyond her son's age and grade levels. Each letter answered specific questions that she would have wondered about for the rest of her life.

While Angela was writing her sons' memorial program, God revealed that their letters were written to soothe her soul, but more importantly to share. She struggled with a new assignment for over five months before she surrendered to the Holy Spirit.

At the time, Angela had fifteen years in the Air Force. She asked God to give her the strength to stay in the military for another five years. If so she would retire and dedicate her life to sharing His amazing testimony. God granted Angela that strength. She spent the next couple of years writing her autobiography title, Miracles in Action ~ Turning Pain into Power and Grief into Power. She retired in 2005 and transferred from military to ministry.

Three years after Murice and Roger passed, the Alexander's social worker called and said she had a fourteen-month little girl who needed a home. Immediately Angela said, "No." Eventually, they compromised. Angela agreed she could come over for a couple of days. God interceded again. Out of all the names in the world, her name is Angela. Out of 365 days of the year, she was placed in their home on April 1, 2003, which was the third anniversary of their sons' passing. With those two major miracles, the Alexanders began adoption paperwork the very next day. Surie laughed and said, "My speech therapist is going to need therapy behind this one!" They believe God said, Surie, my son, you don't have to remember another name. We're gonna ride this Angela train all the way home! All they can say is God has jokes and Miracles are in Action!

Whether you're grieving the passing of your loved one, foreclosure of your home, your health, wealth, marriage, dreams, or expectations. The question is how do you turn your grief into good grief? How do you turn your mourning into good mourning? The answer is you give it to God. When you do, He will turn your pain into power and grief into peace.

ABOUT ANGELA ALEXANDER

On April 1, 2000 while Angela Alexander was in Japan on military duty, her husband and four children were involved in a fatal car crash. The Alexander's car fell twenty-five feet off a California highway, and landed upside down on top of two parked vehicles with people inside. Praise God they were all right! Angela's husband and daughters survived. Sadly, her two eight-year-old sons went home to our Heavenly Father.

Although Murice and Roger passed instantly at the scene, God allowed both to write and leave behind incredible good-bye letters. Murice didn't know about Roger's letter and Roger didn't know about Murice's letter. Both children individually listened to the Holy Spirit and obeyed. Each letter was written above and beyond their age and grade level, and answered specific questions that Angela would have wondered about for the rest of her life. In the letters, she received that peace from God that allowed her to praise His Holy Name. While Angela was writing her sons' memorial program God revealed that their letters were written to soothe her soul, but more importantly to share.

Angela accepted her new assignment and her transition from

military to ministry began. Angela retired from the Air Force in 2005, now she's an Author & Inspirational Speaker of her autobiography titled, *Miracles in Action ~ Turning Pain into Power and Grief into Peace,* and the Executive Producer of *Miracles in Action* the documentary film. Angela is also the co-founder of the ministry, *Helping Hurting Hearts Heal.*

Invite Angela to share *Miracles in Action* at your church, conference, book club, etc. It will truly be an unforgettable event, and a blessing to all who hear her incredible testimony!

CONTACT ANGELA ALEXANDER

Website: Download Angela's Free eBook, *Seven Steps from Grief to Peace* at www.miraclesinaction.com

Email: Angela@MiraclesInAction.com
Phone: 909-296-1273
Facebook: Angela Tayes Alexander
LinkedIn: Angela Alexander
Twitter: Angela Alexander @MiraclesNAction
YouTube: Angela Alexander Miracles in Action

14. YOU ARE WHAT YOU FEAT!
BY TRACEY BOND

It is written: "…So the disciples were saying to one another, "No one brought Him (Jesus) anything to eat, did he?" Jesus said to them, "My food is to do the will of Him who sent Me and to accomplish His work." – The New Testament Gospel of John, Chapter 4, Verse 33-34

Ever on their movements, many wearisome spirit-fed entrepreneurs might find some point in their independent career journeys, that the engine of their visionary vehicles will need a fresh eye change. By this I mean that the eye of a spiritual entrepreneur's visionary mind can rack up invisible miles of mental exertion travel, like in any other vehicle on the move. I believe I experienced such a revelation, refreshing my mind's eye as I wondered about the purpose God had in choosing my birthday on the 007th day of an August (harvest month) by divine intelligent design with a powerful numerical value often connected to completion and a finishing accomplishment in God's Creation.

In this position for purpose glowing forward, I want you to consider my double agent special ops training for finishing what you accomplish well; knowing that your call to entrepreneurship is innately by divine designer calling - as you are made in the image of His Divine Entrepreneurial Model.

It is written that God worked six days in creating the world, but did you recognize it was begun as Vision from His mind? We are spiritually seeded into his glorious Creation plan, and being created from his divine entrepreneurial mind, this is the way we Spirit-fed entrepreneurs also create our good works: from seeded visions into seasons of planting and feast rewards at harvest time! Realizing the day that I was first called to be His Kingdom undercover agent on double-ohh-seventh heaven duty, I voluntarily lost my spirit malnourished mind; for up to that point it had been pre-programmed by world systems, which are mortally crafted in darkness without divine design. The Good News is by grace I found the Spirit mind of Christ, God's only Son, Jesus.

Since Jesus opened my mind to understand scriptural principles for living; my mind is always on active duty now; like a matrix if you will, of up and downloads God's Spirit programs in and out of seasons. If you get where I am flowing with this, then you probably know what it is for 'surf' to always be up with your brainwaves, coming in regularly at a high energy expense. When you're in that critical point where your mental energy is ready to break your circuits, your soul signals that you need refueling, just like a multi-mile driven vehicle. Fuel comes from natural resources, but your fuel as a Spirit-fed entrepreneur must come from SUPER natural resources. To keep your productivity moving to the next milestone destination of accomplishment, you must develop a soul food plan to sustain your mental fuel for your journey. When adversities come and surely they will show up, your strength will be increased by the diet you feed upon. This strength is supernatural and you must have it from a higher food source in order to accomplish your divinely-designed life work.

As a spiritual entrepreneur of almost twenty years I

consciously operate with no reservations whatsoever about establishing my entrepreneurial visions the unique way that I do. That is because I've learned to consistently put in to practice just like a profession, the source of my successions. I've also learned to develop divine strategies for defeating the adversity waged war over my goals planted there on the 'seedbed' of my mind. Merriam Wester defines 'seedbed' as "an area of soil prepared for planting seeds." From a spiritual perspective I choose to define 'seed' as an '…area of soul prepared there for planting God's seeds."

After seasons of special spiritual ops training in seeding from the soul, I know now that I'm better equipped with favor for my entrepreneurial trips, and sustained by Spirit strength to reach my vision goals. I have developed a few spiritual seed-recipes that strengthen my ability to vanquish every enemy of my goal visions. I am nourished by divine resources that assist me in accomplishing the work that I do…and I do it as a fortified victor nourished by the seeds God has root sourced in my soul. I will share these recipes with you so that you will know what to eat, how to conquer your spirit defeat, and definitely how to do it too!

Q: Do you have a divine diet that sustains your strength for the entrepreneur's journey?

Q: Does fast track food leave your vision famished near the finish and void of vitality?

Q: "ARE YOU HUNGRY TO SEE YOUR VISION SEEDED WORKS BRING GLORY TO GOD?"

If you can answer yes to any of these three question, you're in a good place now to get a feeling for what I want to serve you here from this written-vision feasting table. Hunger is a constant sensation for many entrepreneurs to feel, but spiritual entrepreneurs are divinely designed to thrive on supernatural diet. Grocers have no shelves to store the seed nutrients they must feed on to sustain the vitality of their visions to their finish line. So sourcing them reasonably requires soul-searching. Those seeds are the super natural resources of our faith-integration, fueled by the power contained in the living seed of Christ, the living Spirit of God's Word of truth. Each and every time we receive it, believe it, seed and feed it – we are operating in concert with the will of God, by divine design, to bring about our vision fruits for harvest feasting and more specifically, invisible enemy de'FEAT'ing.

A quick internet keyword Google search will show you in about (0.41 seconds) that 'Hunger'* *is a feeling of discomfort or weakness caused by lack of food, coupled with the desire to eat.*

I don't know about you, but I am attracted consciously, emotionally, physically and spiritually to Higher Life and the meaningful purpose behind living it. I'm hungry to accomplish anything God 'seeds' in me that would produce a harvest of good work I can eat from; to be nourished and resourced for more. The divine design nature of this spirit-fed entrepreneurial work that I do, is transformed into multifaceted bread...my source, resources...my refueling and of course my food. I have come to appreciate more and more each day the words of my soul's Lord and Savior Jesus as it is written in my chapter opening quote:

"...So the disciples were saying to one another, "No one brought Him (Jesus) anything to eat, did he?" Jesus said to them, "My food is to do the will of Him who sent Me and to accomplish His work." – The New Testament Gospel of John, Chapter 4, Verse 33-34

I am convinced these words are what set me apart as a divinely designed spirit-fed entrepreneur. My diet is peculiar as the person I accept that I am in that design. It is because I am what I eat, that I deliciously feed on the will of God as my food, which sustains my soul's strength to accomplish His work. There is a scriptural principle written (in the New Testament 2nd Chapter and verse 3 of the Book of Thessalonians) that says "...if a man won't work he should not eat." I find no need to expound further on that simple statement. Whoever spread the foolish rhetoric that life does not come with a guide, carried a lying spirit...and coincidentally in another place it also is written the devil is a liar spirit being.

A truth in our human being is that all hunger is not good to experience, especially if it is the result of lacking well-paid work as a means to earn what one eats. That hunger could feel like emptiness in the natural man (human being) who has yet to be inhabited by the Spirit of God. How much more is the entrepreneur accustomed to a spirit-fed diet? Spiritual hunger is a pre-indicator of a wanting desire for higher nutrients, the demands of the body can feel like vacancy in the soul. The only food that was made to satiate it to fullest is the unadulterated Word of God's truth. To carry out our spiritual work can be considered that spirit-food that fuels our goals. When God's truth gets planted in the minds of men like a 'seed' vision, they will have been given a spiritual ear to hear it beforehand. When believed with faith consistently, season after season, these truth seeds will then start to germinate and go through growth spurts of their own. If these divine seeds of faith are nourished in an ideal climate of relationship that is founded upon believing and accepting, the spiritually seeded Word of God's truth, personal communication with God is initiated like a PR department in the soul. In that place God authors human beings into existence, calling and even communicating their divine entrepreneurial purpose, and visions for faith working toward completion. Divine seeds that mature into conscious ways of envisioning, thinking about and working for what we eat... can be vision clearing. When entrepreneurial vision is clear, life work can be upright adventurous; and the soul of the entrepreneur will be Spirit guided through cycles and seasons of spirit training that start with a vision, seeding, feeding and harvesting...the fruit of it all.

*SEED: The definition of a seed is a structure that contains the embryo of a plant.

This is how gestation occurs in a human pregnancy, starting with a 'seed' (fertilized embryo) that grows into a baby, feeding off the nourishment a mother provides in 3 seasons many of us understand as trimesters. When the baby has everything it needs to thrive outside of the mother's body, the mothers uterine muscle prepares to harvest (or labor as in work) to deliver the baby as the fruit of her womb.

It is also written in the Old Testament book of Psalms 127:3, "Behold, children are a gift of the LORD, The fruit of the womb is a reward."

This is an example of my entrepreneurial process, as a child of God, born again through the womb of His Holy Spirit. I am convinced there is no detachment of a spiritual cord in the womb of the Spirit as long as we remain in faith connection (believing relationship) with our Creator and heavenly Father. I have learned how to cohabitate in a contented relationship with God my Father, who has spiritually constructed a way to not only inhabit, but sit in the throne room seat of my soul.

The fulfilling relationship I share with God has changed my taste buds for life purpose; I consciously dine with divine diet in mind, with a peculiar palate for Son-flowered seeds that Spirit sprouts in the seedbed of my soul. Spirit does the gardening and resourcing and brings forth my mature fruit at the 'ripe' time of harvest: allowing me to feast over the reward, like the gestating woman does over her baby, the fruit from her womb.

My spiritual seed diet is watered and Son 'lit' by faith in the truth of God's Word, and the harvest reward season's bottom line will surely top off to overflow. Why? The seed that you vision plan & Spirit plant in order to eat, will bring forth fruit despite adversity, ripened on the vine, divine and sweet! That is what we can consider a goal achieved and a rewarding accomplishment. A word that also means to perform successfully or my chosen word, 'feat.'

Q: Did you know each time you perform a divinely designed entrepreneurial 'feat,' a powerful advertisement loops in the realms of spirit atmospheres from Heaven to Hell? Yes…a voice that is ever vetting you as "more than a conqueror," touting your victories as fruitfully sweet. You can believe it is true, because the Spirit of Almighty God, the source and seed you feed upon, continues to breed and bring forth this fruit from the spirit-entrepreneurial-womb of you. You will have proven to God and your adversities, that you consistently 'become what you eat' and you have 'overcome what you defeat.'

When you are rewarded at the time of your entrepreneurial task completion with a harvest so abundant, that you need more than the two hands God has given to help you harvest it, you will want to glorify Him through your fruit, effortlessly. If you have a revelation of what I just shared, let me shout AMEN with you right there and take a moment to bless God for your Spirit-fed entrepreneurship. This is your high-powered calling to marketplace ministry…to God be the all the Glory for His wonderful works!

As you continue to endeavor in meaningful entrepreneurial work of higher purpose that brings forth the will of God in your life, be encouraged in knowing that you are glorifying God by the fruit you bear from this unique career lifestyle, in season and out.

It is written where Jesus Our Lord and Savior said in John 15: 8

"If you abide in Me, and My words abide in you, ask whatever you wish, and it will be done for you. "My Father is glorified by this, that you bear much fruit, and so prove to be My disciples. "Just as the Father has loved Me, I have also loved you; abide in My love…"   –Jesus

Living in the love of my Heavenly Father sustains the source of everything I need to accomplish the work I have been sent to do. The seed of His Word of Truth I feed on. It produces a harvest variety of abundance in my life and my entrepreneurial works.

The harvest is plenty and the laborers are few. We who

have taken on this great work in the harvest fields of God's Creation, know the seed is the source we must patiently bring forth to keep us fed in so many ways. We must harvest it, replant it and share it with men and continue this process over again and over again. We must also keep in mind that just as every soil area of seed planting has its own natural enemies, spirit-fed entrepreneurs will have them too. We must actively guard the visions God plants into our supernatural seedbeds, to work into fruition. We must become what we eat as seed and win our food fights of our souls.

The divine diet we have is designed to strengthen us for these soul food fights, as the Word of God we believe prevents us from forfeiting our vision goals. We are more than conquering entrepreneurs at fighting for that which threatens the resources of our feed. I am proud to share my spirit-fed seedbed recipes. If only more of natural men would taste them and 'seed' how good they can be.

When the vision-seeded goals you have hungrily eaten, and worked through Spirit to completion, come near their harvest season/feast time; adversity may get thirsty for a spirit fight dark-and-dirty, and food-fight your inner light for a 'gladuation' seat...fork your mind full of ease with these seed recipes...and defeat your seed source enemies with the knowledge:

"YOU ARE WHAT YOU FEAT!"

ABOUT TRACEY BOND

Tracey is an emergent double Press agent/PR solopreneur, who serves extraordinary clientele with award-winning talents & multi-industry skills at her Beverly Hills launched Beneficience.com Prolific Personage PR operative and mediaphilic ™ prodcast ™ show "SPEAK! @intothePODlight" on BlogTalkRadio. Bond entertains her fond description as an online media industry's 'Olivia (PR)ope of PR hope...and scope!'

Daily Tracey can be found sweet-spotting the spotlight online to offline for her clients by introducing, sourcing, sporting and courting their personage & perceptions with her niche for digital brand journalistic selections.

As a VIP journalist, Bond's Top 10 U.S. Press Agency's VIP news & social intelligence news beat is globally distributed to thousands of intentional readers and trends-to-spotlight the sensible events and interests of: VIP, Celebrities, Lifestyle & Society, Social Business Event News, Celebrities, Entertainment and Online Media centric to social good.

Moving forward via this double press agency/pr platform, Bond continues to build an elite clientele base upon her personable media brand showcase of high-profile digital brand journalism, speaking and publicity all which carry an authentic & distinctive trifecta of marketable excellence.

As an author however: Bond is purposed to continue publishing nonfiction books, niche industry teaching tools and other multimedia assets toward humanitarian interests such as: "Kingdom Of God Gold Digger: Mining The Golden Treasury Of A Rich Inheritance Found Only In God; Face Booking U: A VIP Face Publishing School Imparting New Values of Fame, Frame & Fortune As VIP Social Networthing ™ Public Relations Tools

CONTACT TRACEY BOND

Booking/Media/Opportunities & Engagements Information

Publicity email: tracey@beneficiencepublicrelations.com
Author Email: traceybond007@gmail.com
Phone: (707) 271-6171 Extension #2 {Direct}
Mobile: (815) 375-4286
Twitter: @tracey007bond
Instagram: https://www.instagram.com/traceybond007
Website: http://TraceyBond007.com
Blog: TraceyBond007.com
LinkedIn:
https://www.linkedin.com/in/traceybonddoubleohhseven

15. PAUSE
BY MELINDA DAY-HARPER

"He who can no longer pause to wonder and stand rapt in awe, is as good as dead; his eyes are closed." -- *Albert Einstein*

As I sit here on my porch looking out over the beautiful Texas Hill Country, the ***Power of Pause*** strikes me. I've spent a lifetime as a Human Doing more often than a Human Being. Now, I'll grant you that served me fairly well for the most part; it was my survival technique. Maybe you can relate?

I lost seven family members from 1984 to 1987, including the tragic accident that took the life of my sister's husband of three months, the unexpected death of my father-in-law, the 1985 brutal murder of my Dad, at the age of 54, and the subsequent murder trial and my grandfather's massive heart attack shortly after. In a six-week period in 1995, my dear grandmother Nan had a stroke and died, my Mom had brain surgery to remove a large tumor, my sister had breast surgery, my brother, at the age of 44, was accidentally electrocuted to death, and I was named President-CEO of a national company. In 2005, my Mom died, I had to prepare for the first parole hearing of my Dad's murderer, and my sister was in a drug-induced coma for three days (what would become an annual occurrence). In 2008, my 19-year old nephew died of a drug overdose. In 2012, being the only surviving next of kin, I had to tell the neurologist to go ahead and pull the plug on my 49-year-old sister after her liver failure. There have been many others, family, and friends.

Yikes! These few details of my life seem unbelievable when I see them all written. The three therapists I have seen each told me they'd never heard anything like it – so NOT helpful, I told them that and never **went** back! Throughout most of those times, there was no time to grieve. I became the family's funeral/eulogy expert and have become quite good at dealing with that process. I became a Human Doing so I could keep my grief and accompanying emotions in their place – my mental "file drawer" (which eventually became a Vault) where I could file them away hopefully never to be felt again.

I kept talking to God the first ten years or so with the first 'wave' of tragedies, but towards the end of that time, I really don't think He was too pleased with what He was hearing. I was angry. Very angry. And it was all His fault for letting these things happen TO ME! Because it was always about ME, right? I relived those events over and over in my head day after day and shut God out. I didn't need Him; He wasn't fixing things; He wasn't helping; He wasn't doing what I wanted Him to do – to make it Stop. So I just kept Doing.

Today, I am so very grateful for the blessings I've been given, for the time I have (however long or short) with family and friends, my fur kids, my career, and mostly for my **peace.** I spend time every single morning thanking God and asking Him to guide my thoughts, actions, and words so that I may do His will, not mine. He answers. I am at **Peace**. *How did I get Here from There?*

Well, first I decided I would just take control and handle things all on my own. After all, the God Plan wasn't working out so well, or so I thought. Good Lord, what a mess I made! I was miserable; bad things kept happening, and my mental file cabinet was overflowing. Emotions were leaking out in spurts faster than I could deal with them. Well, as you can imagine, the "Me Plan" worked out even worse than I thought the "God Plan" had. Eventually, I reached the point where I no longer cared if I woke up in the morning. In fact, when I did wake up, I was frequently disappointed. Reaching the point where I truly wanted to die was devastating. I was always the one person that stepped up, took care of things for everyone and carried on. I couldn't do it anymore.

Desperate, I finally just gave up. I sincerely asked Him for guidance and help. He gave it to me. He gave me a *Pause.* He gave me a Time Out – time to put my life back together, time to learn to deal with my grief and anger, and most importantly, time to reconnect with Him. There was (is!) nothing obscuring the direct communication line between Him and me anymore. It quite literally saved my life.

This was a step at a time process, learning to trust God, keeping life *simple* enough to remember where "my" power comes from, taking a frequent *Pause* to reconnect with nature, with God, with myself. I find today that what had to be a conscious effort at first on my part has now become intuitive. When negative thoughts creep in or I find myself getting agitated or annoyed or feeling useless or ("fill in the blank"), I *Pause* and ask Him for guidance and peace. He answers. Simple, really.

It has been said that God puts situations in our lives to deal with, that point us toward our Purpose. If mine is to be a funeral director, I think I've got it now! But no, I don't believe that's it. I believe that my Purpose is to Lighten Life's Load© for others. Period. However, and whenever I can with the talents and skill sets He has given me. That's cool! He has given me a good mind for business, an affinity with numbers and a desire to help others Lighten Life's Load© by keeping things simple. I use those gifts today and remain mindful of them, so I can stay on track with what I'm here for.

Pause serves me well in my career as a business consultant. Can you remember getting so passionate about a particular issue/circumstance that you basically just opened your mouth, and all this "stuff" came spewing out? "Stuff" that you immediately wished you hadn't said? "Stuff" that once said, was not helpful to the situation; perhaps it was even detrimental to your goals. We can get so caught up in the "drama" created by others and ourselves because we are all passionate about our beliefs. That's all well and good, but must be tempered with a sincere desire to understand another's viewpoint; to truly Pause our minds, our thinking about our own opinions and listen. Sometimes, we're wrong and can actually learn useful things from others – what a concept!

I'm grateful for how He sometimes reminds me to *Pause* – for example, looking for one of my fur kids and finding him like this:

Buck floated in the pool for almost an hour, perfectly still, perfectly intent on watching birds and butterflies, just perfectly, peacefully, *Pawsing!* Aaaah, a lesson graciously taught, gratefully learned.

The obstacles put in my path, no matter their source, invite me to grow, to move beyond my current thinking and consider other alternatives. They offer me chances to be the woman I was meant to be – courageous and confident - as long as I can *Pause* long enough to let my 'guard' take a break and just be a Human Being. Just for Today. Just for This Moment. I am at Peace. I am connected with God, and I am connected with all of you. We are all on this Journey together. I find comfort in that. So, just for Today, take a few moments to *Pause,* be peacefully connected with everything around you. There you will Find Your Purpose and Live Your Passion©.

ABOUT MELINDA DAY-HARPER

Melinda has over 25 years' experience in senior and executive corporate management. A CPA and CGMA by profession ("but not by personality", she says), Melinda has coached hundreds of employees to excellence in her roles as CFO of a number of large companies, CEO of a multi-million-dollar enterprise, award-winning speaker, and best-selling author. She founded T-Zone Consulting in 2006 to help others *Break Boundaries* and design their own lives. Her speaking skills have captivated and entertained thousands! Melinda is a member of IAC, IACCW, NAWBO, AICPA and TSCPA.

Melinda is also a freelance musician, known as Queen B (Bass guitarist and Backup vocals)! She enjoys playing with her many dogs, cats and other critters on her Texas Hill Country ranch. **Her passion is to Lighten Life's Load for others as they find their way through this journey of Life.**

CONTACT MELINDA DAY-HARPER

Website: www.TZoneConsulting.com
Facebook: www.facebook.com/TZoneConsulting
LinkedIn: www.linkedin.com/in/mdayharper
Phone: (210) 867-7286

16. SPIRIT FED ENTREPRENEUR: GROW YOUR BUSINESS WITH A FEARLESS MINDSET
BY JAYNE RIOS

So many times I have been asked, "How do you incorporate God into your business?" My answer is, "We all have a gift, we all have a passion, now combine those and you have a business with PURPOSE." When I was in Africa, God showed me that eLearning would be beneficial to missionaries, but after researching the opportunity 10 years ago, it was too expensive. I knew God wanted this, so I found someone who created a low-cost eLearning system in the States and repackaged it to missionaries. Because of this act of Faith and moving on His instruction, I was able to work with one of the largest ministries in the World. God's eLearning system saved them time, money, travel and in some cases the missionaries life. There are 7 underground churches learning online in China because I listened, acted and combined my skill set and passion to serve Him. And I give Him all the Glory!

I wasn't always like this, so how did I get fearless and learn to listen and take action? Below are 10 steps that will help!

Step 1: Self Accountability

"Do not conform to the pattern of this world, but be transformed by the renewing of your mind." Romans 12: 1

Why is this first? Only you can control the "unhealthy fear" thoughts in your head. Only you know what you are thinking at any given time. Only you can begin to stop and turn your thinking around. So self-accountability is so important; it is the NUMBER one step to having a fearless mindset. You must take the responsibility and you must control yourself. The only way to turn it around is to know that you are PROTECTED and LOVED by the GOD who made the earth and most importantly made YOU with a PURPOSE!

If you do not know that you are a child of God, simply ask Jesus to come into your heart and to be your Lord and Savior (for those already saved, please read on but I thought this was so important to talk about before moving into the steps for living without fear and leading a Spirit Fed Life.) For those who would like to KNOW they are saved and protected by God, please pray the prayer below and get into a Bible-based Church. You will meet some great new friends and it will help you along to live the Spirit Fed life you are so desiring! Read the sinner's prayer below to KNOW that you are saved and to begin your Spirit Fed journey with the One who created the universe…God and with His Son…Jesus!

Salvation Prayer

Jesus I know that we are all sinners and I am alienated from God and His protection, I realize I cannot save myself and only through believing that your Son Jesus Christ died on the cross for me and my sins can I be saved. God I believe in your Son and I ask you to come into my Heart and be my Lord and Savior. Amen

The Bible reads you are saved and that the Holy Spirit now lives inside of you and will Guide your path. So let's turn any negative thinking into positive, encouraging and uplifting thoughts.

10 Tips to Eliminate Negative Thinking

Below are 10 tips to overcome negative thinking, try them out. This is your homework for this week!

1. Read the verses in the back of this book and memorize a few to remind yourself throughout the day who you REALLY are!

2. Meditation/Yoga

3. Smile

4. Surround yourself with ONLY positive people

5. Change the tone of your thoughts from negative to positive (wear a rubber band around your wrist and every time you have a negative thought, POP yourself and turn it into something positive or something you are grateful for.)

6. Help someone else

7. Sing

8. Watch a funny TV show or movie

9. List 3 things you are grateful for

10. Read positive affirmations or quotes

Step 2: Love Yourself

"Love is patient, kind, does not envy, does not boast, is not proud, is not rude, is not self-seeking, is not easily angered, keeps no record of wrongs...LOVE never fails."   *– 1 Corinthians*

Read the scripture above…do you love YOURSELF like this? If the answer is no, then that's our second step. It's hard to live a Spirit Fed life unless you are living this within yourself.

Be patient with yourself, your life, your business, etc. Be still and take time to listen. It's amazing when you take just 5 minutes in the morning to be still and ask for guidance, the answers do come…but you have to be patient and be still and hear.

Be kind to yourself. Quit beating yourself up for past mistakes. Take time to look and feel good. Take time for yourself, whatever it is you like doing, do it. Celebrate your life!

Be grateful for what you have and do not envy what others have. You never know what's happening behind the facade and closed doors. What seems like paradise might be pure hell. Don't compare yourself and don't covet. Be grateful for you and your surroundings.

Be humble, don't be proud. This means don't let your ego get in the way. Stay humble. Authenticity is key.

Be nice, don't be rude. A Spirit Fed person puts others needs before their own. Give people a break, we are only human. And remember what Mom told you…" if you don't have anything nice to say, please don't say anything at all". We are all trying our best with our given circumstances. Do you tell yourself this? Don't beat yourself up. Be nice to yourself.

Serve others, stop being self-seeking. When you only serve yourself, you will end up by yourself. Spirit Fed people serve others with an open heart. We all need each other at one point or another.

Control your anger. Control your tongue. Get a system in place for when you feel the anger arising you have a plan. Walk away, pop yourself with a rubber band on your wrist…whatever it is, stay calm. Learn to control your anger, it serves no one any good, especially you!

Keep no record of wrong. Forgiveness is a big step. You are only hurting yourself. People make mistakes, granted some are bigger than others. However, this is one of the biggest roadblocks in leading a Spirit Fed life. Forgive yourself!

Love never fails! These are each areas you can work on to lead a Spirit Fed life this year.

Step 3: Know Thyself

"Since we have these promises, beloved, let us cleanse ourselves from every defilement of body and spirit, bringing holiness to completion in the fear of God." -2 Corinthians 7:1

Knowing thyself is critical. Again, only you know you better than anyone on this earth. You know what makes you happy and you know what makes you tick or angry. Begin taking inventory!

Keep a list of what makes you tick and create a plan to counter balance your anger with something positive. This takes practice, but when you know what makes you angry, you can control it.

Also make a list of what makes you happy. In those moments of despair and depression, get your list out and make an effort to change your mindset. Also memorize some of the Scripture in the back of the book and remind yourself daily.

Lastly make a list of everything GREAT about you! This is the list we are going to tape to our mirrors around the house and stick in our purses and briefcases. When you begin to fear or think negatively about yourself, get that piece of paper out…READ IT…. OWN IT!

Step 4: Be Ready to Forgive

"Love keeps no record of wrong." -1 Corinthians 13:5

"And forgive us our debts, as we also have forgiven our debtors." – Matthew 6:12

Forgiveness is a big step for many of us. Why should we forgive? Because it's holding you back. Unforgiveness brings about anger, tears, depression, hate and so many other emotions. The crazy thing is, it holds *us* down, *not* the person who angered us. So it's a MUST if you are ready to live a Spirit Fed life to FORGIVE anyone or anything that might have hurt you…no matter what it is!

You may never forget, but there won't be that burning feeling of anger and resentment in your soul every time you think about it. You have to let it go in order to move forward. If you need to forgive yourself for something, it's the same process. But you should go to that person in love and apologize…even if they do not accept, you have done what you can. Now let God take over to change the other person's heart.

How do you forgive? You simply acknowledge you were hurt. You could approach the person who hurt you and let them know how you feel and hope for an apology to make you feel better but in most incidences you won't get that apology which only makes you angrier. I suggest you write down your hurts on one side of the paper on the other side write down how it affected you. Now FORGIVE and MOVE on! It sounds simplistic, and it is. Some hurts are bigger than others, but forgiveness is the same whether big or small.

Stop thinking about who or how you were hurt, it's over. At this point take control of your own life and move forward my friend.

Step 5: Stay Determined

"A hard worker has plenty of food, but a person who chases fantasies has no sense." – Proverbs 12:11

It takes determination to a live a Spirit Fed, fearless life. You have to tell yourself…I fear no evil, I fear nobody, I fear nothing. How can you do this? Your Faith that God has something so great for you that you don't have time to waste! Fear will keep you back, be DETERMINED to move forward!

Be determined to make a difference today! Let go of self-doubt and the voices in your head telling you that you are not good enough. Listen to what God says, read HIS WORD every day!

What makes the winners different from the 'others'? Determination! Everybody dreams, but people who actually fulfill their dreams is a totally a different thing.

Step 1: Manage your time. No matter how hard you try, if you don't know how to manage your time, then success is a long road for you. So try managing your time efficiently. Make a chart and start keeping track of your time during the day. Re-evaluate at the end of the week and determine what you can do to manage time more efficiently…rinse and repeat!

Step 2: Make a To-do List. Make a list of the things required to do. Don't make your list an impossible thing to achieve by including everything to do in a single day. If you have items left over on your list from the day, simply carry them over to your list for tomorrow! Don't beat yourself up because you didn't complete them. Tomorrow is a new day. You will get it done because you have…DETERMINATION!

Step 3: Give yourself time to reflect over the day. Were you able to complete the tasks? Or was something left-out? If yes, then why? Soon by answering these questions you'll become efficient at accomplishing every single task in your list.

Step 4: Have confidence in yourself. Changes are uncomfortable. And we humans have a tendency to avoid changes and ignore them as much as possible. But if you want to achieve something, you'll have to break the comfortable shell of yours. If you face failures in the beginning, don't let them discourage you. Try and try until you succeed.

Step 5: Strengthen the Muscle of Determination: We fail to meet our goals because our power of determination is weak. Like a muscle that we've never exercised, we get tired out easily and the enthusiasm we started out with, quickly fizzles. And what's more, failing to attain a goal can be discouraging, making it more difficult to attempt something challenging in the future. **But determination is not something you're born with**, nor is it simply a choice you can make in an instant. Rather, this is a power that must be nurtured and developed over a period of time. Interestingly enough, the process of intelligent goal-setting is itself an excellent means of cultivating determination.

Step 6: Get Focused

"Since we have been justified through faith, we have peace with God through our Lord Jesus Christ." – Romans 5:1

Knowing this scripture above, you can focus on what needs to be done. Jesus died for our sins/worries, so we didn't have to fear or worry. He promises to care for us in ALL situations. When you TRULY and FULLY understand this, you can FOCUS on what needs to be done!

Create a list of your focus points: need to forgive someone, need to work on anger, need to make more money, whatever it is. Second step is to prioritize the list and work on one thing at a time, using COMPLETE FOCUS! Once you conquer one, move to the next.

If you are having trouble focusing, ask God for His help. He will help you in whatever area of life you are needing help. I want you to Focus on leading a Spirit Fed, fearless life. Get past everything you fear that's holding you back, take care of it so you can move forward! Get clear about what you want! What you focus on is what you get! Put a plan together and set it in motion today. It's NEVER too late.

In order to focus, you have to have an end result. What are you focused on? That's your end result. And the fastest way to get the end result is to create an action plan.

In some ways, an action plan is a "heroic" act: it helps us turn our dreams into a reality. An action plan is a way to make sure your vision, coupled with your complete focus is made concrete. It describes the way you will use the strategies to meet the objectives. An action plan consists of a number of action steps or changes to be brought about in your thoughts, movements and day-to-day activities.

Step 7: Have Faith in Yourself

"Trust in the Lord with all your heart, and do not lean on your own understanding. In all your ways acknowledge him, and he will make straight your paths." — Proverbs 3:5-6

Sometimes we are just too hard on ourselves, have Faith in yourself. You have made it this far and you have so much more to do! Believe in yourself. Everyone has something they have gone through that can help someone else.

Take out a piece of paper and in the first column I want you to write down everything you are good at, reasons why you love yourself, all your good qualities. Really think about this and write down everything! You will reference this list often to remember who you are! When you are Spirit Fed and fearless, you KNOW your strengths, you KNOW your weaknesses and you have confidence!

In the next column write down everything that God says you are in Him:

Child of the Highest God

Protected

Loved

Forgiven

Blessed

He sent His Son to die for us, that's HOW MUCH HE LOVES YOU! Have faith in yourself. Love and seek God with all of your heart, soul and mind and everything else will be added unto you!

Step 8: Get Up and Move

"How long will you sleep? When will you wake up? A little extra sleep, a little extra slumber – then poverty will pounce on you like a bandit; scarcity will attack you like an armed robber."
– Proverbs 6:9

Fear holds us back from our greatness. Many times you just need to get up and move and God can do the rest! Have you ever heard the following saying? If opportunity doesn't knock, build a door.

I can't tell you how many people I coach who have such a great opportunity, but their fear of reaching beyond their comfort zone is paralyzing. If God put a dream or idea in your heart, don't stop at anything until it comes to pass. God says He is there for us; all we have to do is call on Him. But God can't interfere unless we ask, that's what we call Free Will! Same thing, if you are in your house afraid to move, or afraid to go to networking events, or afraid to pick up the phone and call, God helps but is limited by your unwillingness to move. It is up to you to GET UP AND MOVE! I always tell people for every step I make, God moves ten!

Make a list today of everything you would really like to do if you actually could make it happen, this is your vision list, keep it and refer to it often. You can make this happen if you get up with fearlessness!

Step 9: Speak Up!

"Don't worry about anything; instead pray about everything.
Tell God what you need, and thank Him for all He has done.
Then you will experience God's peace, which exceeds anything
we can understand. His peace will guard your hearts and minds
as you live in Christ Jesus." – Philippians 4:6-7

This is a direct quote from the Bible. Either you believe it or not! Now is the time to re-read that verse and OWN IT! If God says He'll deliver, but you have to ask and believe, then and only then, will you receive. When you really know this in your heart, you can live a Spirit Fed, fearless life.

Too many times we think what we want is trivial or too small or selfish. God wants you to be fully alive, happy and live in abundance. He wants to help you. If your child asked for a steak, would you give him a raw fish? NO…just like we want the best for our kids, God wants the best for us. But we have to ask. God gave us free will, so He will not intercede *unless* we speak up.

Free Will

God dignifies us with free will, the power to make decisions of our own rather than having God or fate predetermine what we do. Consider what the Bible teaches.

- ***God created humans in his image. (Genesis 1:26)*** Unlike animals, which act mainly on instinct, we resemble our Creator in our capacity to display such qualities as love and justice. And like our Creator, we have free will.

- To a great extent, we can determine our future. The Bible encourages us to "choose life . . . by listening to [God's] voice," that is, by choosing to obey his commands. (Deuteronomy 30:19,

20) This offer would be meaningless, even cruel, if we lacked free will. Instead of forcing us to do what he says, God warmly appeals to us: *"O if only you would actually pay attention to my commandments! Then your peace would become just like a river." (Isaiah 48:18)*.

- Our success or failure is not determined by fate. If we want to succeed at an endeavor, we must work hard. "All that your hand finds to do," says the Bible, "do with your very power." (Ecclesiastes 9:10) It also says: *"The plans of the diligent one surely make for advantage." (Proverbs 21:5)*.

Free will is a precious gift from God, for it lets us love him with our "whole heart"—because we want to. (Matthew 22:37).

Doesn't God control all things?

The Bible does teach that God is Almighty, that His power is not limited by anyone other than Himself. (Job 37:23; Isaiah 40:26) However, He does not use His power to control everything. For example, the Bible says that God was "exercising self-control" toward ancient Babylon, an enemy of his people. (Isaiah 42:14) Similarly, for now, He chooses to tolerate those who misuse their free will to harm others. But God will not do so indefinitely. (Psalm 37:10, 11).

So we must SPEAK UP and ask God to help in ALL things! Don't try and handle things yourself. Don't wait until you're in the middle of a problem to ask. Ask before the problem arises. He is waiting for you to ASK, but because of free will all He can do is watch as you try and handle things on your own. Speaking up is critical! Pray!

Step 10: Surround Yourself with Good People

**"Do not be misled: Bad company corrupts good character." –
1 Corinthians 5:33**

Leading a Spirit Fed, fearless life on your own is more difficult
when you don't have GREAT, supportive, positive people around
you. Finding great friends with your same belief system goes a
LONG way! Join groups with like-minded individuals, reach out
to your community and find organizations that support your goals.
When you hang out with a negative, unsupportive crowd, it begins
to weigh on you. Find others who will support you on your Spirit
Fed journey.

I dare to say you may need to end some friendships that aren't
beneficial. Make a list of all of your "friends" and "family", and
place a check by those who lift you up in life, spend your energy
there. For the others, limit your time. If you are living with
someone negative, make a list of everything that bothers you about
this person and begin to pray for a change…God does miracles
every day, today may be their day. Always know when you are
with someone negative, you can remain peaceful. Who knows, you
may be a great influence on them.

ABOUT THE COMPILER JAYNE RIOS

Jayne Rios has 25 years' experience in TV and marketing. She is the CEO & co-Founder of WGLA: Women's Global Leadership Alliance, President and Founder of WBTVN Women's Broadcast Television Network and CEO and Founder of Spirit Fed Institute. She is passionate about helping others achieve the success she has earned.

Jayne is author of The Interactive Author: Monetize Your Message, compiler and author of Spirit Fed Entrepreneur and co-author of Pure Wealth, Networking to Increase Your Net Worth, The Unsinkabable Soul and Change Your World.

For anyone ready to incorporate God into their business or those who are ready to eliminate unhealthy fear and move forward visit http://www.spiritfedlife.com.

CONTACT JAYNE RIOS

Begin living the life you want, visit our website for a free offer: http://www.spiritfedbook.com or to host your own television show within our Spirit Fed Network visit http://www.womensbroadcasttv.com.

Contact Links:

Email: jayne@godfident.com

Phone: 817-480-3485

Websites: http://www.spiritfedlife.com and http://www.womensgla.com and http://www.womensbroadcasttv.com

Facebook:

Like our Page at: https://www.facebook.com/spiritfedmindset

Visit Jayne's personal page and connect at: https://www.facebook.com/acts2technology and join our Global Network at: https://www.facebook.com/groups/womensgloballeadershipallianc e/

Twitter: http://www.twitter.com/SpiritFedLife

LinkedIn: http://www.linkedin.com/in/jaynerios

SPIRIT FED SCRIPTURE

I want to remind you right now who GOD is. He wants you to have BIG FAITH and ask for BIG THINGS! He is God Almighty my friends.

Let me tell you a quick story. We visited Cancun this summer with my boys, 10 and 12 years old. When we arrived to the beach there was seaweed everywhere along the shoreline. I prayed that night that God would blow the seaweed away and that we would have a clear beach on our vacation. The next morning, you guessed it, the seaweed was gone, it was out toward the middle of the ocean. It was a great lesson for my boys to know how powerful our God is and how He loves to show us GREAT and MIGHTY things…but we have to ask AND believe!

Scripture to Increase Faith

Deuteronomy 7:9 | Know therefore that the LORD thy God, he is God, the faithful God, which keepeth covenant and mercy with them that love him and keep his commandments to a thousand generations;

Luke 17:5 | And the apostles said unto the Lord, Increase our faith.

Luke 17:6 | the Lord said, If ye had faith as a grain of mustard seed, ye might say unto this sycamore tree, Be thou plucked up by the root, and be thou planted in the sea; and it should obey you.

Luke 17:19 | And he said unto him, Arise, go thy way: thy faith that made thee whole.

Luke 18:8 | tell you that he will avenge them speedily. Nevertheless when the Son of man cometh, shall he find faith on the earth?

Luke 18:42 | And Jesus said unto him, receive thy sight: thy faith that saved thee

Luke 19:17 | And he said unto him, Well, thou good servant: because thou hast been faithful in a very little, have thou authority over ten cities.

Luke 22:32 | But I have prayed for thee, that thy faith fail not: and when thou art converted, strengthen thy brethren.

Acts 6:8 | And Stephen, full of faith and power, did great wonders and miracles among the people.

Acts 11:24 | For he was a good man, and full of the Holy Ghost and of faith: and much people was added unto the Lord.

About Spirit Fed Institute and Spirit Fed Life

Want to Succeed as a Spiritual Life Coach or Integrate Spirituality into Your Business?

The Spirit Fed Institute is the world's leading spiritual coaching training center for transformational coaching. We provide all the resources, education, kits, and preparation you need to become trained and certified!

- Do you know your purpose is to help others discover their dreams, and you want to incorporate spirituality into your program?
- Do you have a desire to help others create a life they love living?

- Is your deepest longing to make the world a better place by living your purpose as a speaker, teacher, and coach and you know that spirituality is a big part of that but you aren't sure how to create a business with it?

Then I have good news for you. You're in the right place!

We specialize in certifying heart-centered, difference makers. Our proven transformational programs developed by Spirit Fed Life founder Jayne Rios have been the top choice of cutting-edge coaches internationally.

Even more, what sets us apart from ordinary life coach training and certification is that we offer you a proven business model to attract and enroll clients… so you can be successful from the start!

www.spiritfedlife.com